COPTIC PARADIGMS

GREGORY E. STERLING

COPTIC PARADIGMS

A Summary of Sahidic Coptic Morphology

PEETERS
LEUVEN - PARIS - WALPOLE, MA
2008

Library of Congress Cataloging-in-Publication Data

Sterling, Gregory E.
Coptic paradigms: a summary of Sahidic Coptic morphology / Gregory E. Sterling.
p. cm.
Tables and glossaries of Coptic forms with English introd., notes, and equivalents.
Supplement to Thomas Oden Lambdin's Introduction to Sahidic Coptic.
Includes bibliographical references.
ISBN-13: 978-90-429-1872-6 (alk. paper)
1. Sahidic dialect–Morphology. I. Lambdin, Thomas Oden. Introduction to Sahidic Coptic. II. Title.

PJ2059.S74 2007
493'.2--dc22

2006047829

D. 2008/0602/150
ISBN 978-90-429-1872-6

INTRODUCTION

Facility in reading an ancient language requires several competencies: control of the morphology, a working vocabulary of common words and phrases, and a grasp of the syntax. Morphology and vocabulary are largely a matter of memorization, although reading always demands textual skills. Syntax is often more challenging. There is, however, a relation among the three. Mastery of the morphology and vocabulary of a language make it possible to concentrate on the syntax. The less effort that a student must devote to the form of a word or the possible meanings of a word or phrase, the greater the likelihood that he or she will be able to make her or his way through even the most difficult syntactical constructions with some dexterity. Conversely, the more that a student struggles with forms or resorts to a lexicon, the less likely it is that the student will be able to solve complex syntactical constructions. The degree of difficulty rises exponentially as a student comes to grips with combinations of morphology, lexicography, and syntax. This small pedagogical aide is devoted to the morphology of Sahidic Coptic. It is thus intended to address one dimension for those who want to read Sahidic Coptic.

This work arose in the context of teaching Coptic to students at the University of Notre Dame. While there are a number of full grammars available, there is a need for a summary of Coptic morphology that brings together all of the basic forms in a convenient layout. Beginning students often find it useful to see the whole of a part of speech at a glance as they learn discrete units. For example, I have found it helpful to explain the Coptic verbal system as a whole as students begin to work their way through specific conjugations. A few minutes with a chart that lays out the differences between sentence and clause conjugations in the tripartite verbal system immediately clarifies the basic concepts. Again, students need an explanation of the system of conversion in Coptic. I think that it is important to give students an overview of the conversion system at a relatively early stage and to repeat and expand it as they advance through the grammar. Similarly, students often find a chart that lists the various pronouns in one convenient place to be helpful. It permits them to see the range of forms and how the specific paradigm that they are learning relates to paradigms of other pronouns. It also allows them to review the paradigms that they have learned to date. This little aide is intended to help beginning students see the whole of Coptic morphology at a glance. I assume that beginning students who use this book, will use it in conjunction with an introductory grammar. It is not a grammar and should not be used as a substitute for a full grammar. I have developed it as a supplement to a very fine grammar:

Thomas O. Lambdin, *Introduction to Sahidic Coptic*. Macon, GA: Mercer University Press, 1983.

It may also be used with a more recent grammar that appeared as this work was in page proofs:

Bentley Layton, *Coptic in 20 Lessons: Introduction to Sahidic Coptic With Exercises & Vocabularies*. Leuven - Paris - Dudley: Peeters, 2007.

There is a second group of students who may also find this tool useful. Coptic is typically a third or fourth ancient language for students. Most students will not become Coptologists, but will need to be able to read texts from the Nag Hammadi corpus or from early Christian writers. They tend to do this sporadically after their formal course work. If the time lapses between readings are too long, they lose their grip on the language and find it painful to work through a text. They do not need to begin anew, but to review their knowledge of morphology. This work is intended to help them. I routinely require students to review Coptic morphology systematically as they begin reading Coptic texts.

The purposes of the work have controlled its scope: it is not exhaustive, but complete enough that it provides broad coverage of most possible forms. I have made the most of the conventions that appear in introductory grammars (but not in actual texts) in an effort to be clear. For example, I have used — to set off distinct morphemes as a way to help students recognize the distinctive elements of a word.

In developing this supplement, I have drawn from a range of grammars and monographs. These include the following:

Bentley Layton. *A Coptic Grammar: With Chrestomathy and Glossary (Sahidic Dialect)*. Porta linguarum orientalium, Neue Serie 20. Wiesbaden: Harrasowitz, 2000, 2004[2].

Alexis Mallon, *Grammaire Copte: Bibliographie, chrestomathie, et vocabulaire*. Beyrouth: Imprimerie catholique, 1956[4].

Chris H. Reintges. *Coptic Egyptian (Sahidic Dialect): A Learner's Grammar*. Afrikawissenschaftliche Lehrbücher 15. Köln: Rüdiger Köppe, 2004.

Ariel Shisha-Halevy, *Coptic Grammatical Categories: Structural Studies in the Syntax of Shenoutean Sahidic*. Analecta Orientalia 53. Rome: Pontificium Institutum Biblicum, 1986.

——. *Coptic Grammatical Chrestomathy: A Course for Academic and Private Study*. Orientalia Lovaniensia Analecta 30. Leuven: Peeters, 1988.
Georg Steindorff, *Lehrbuch der koptischen Grammatik.* Chicago: University of Chicago, 1951.
W.C. Till, *Koptisches Grammatik (saïdischer Dialekt) mit Bibliographie, Lesestucken und Worterverzeichnissen.* 2nd ed. Leipzig: Harrassowitz, 1961.
J. Vergote. *Grammaire copte. I: Introduction, phonetique et phonologie, morphologie synthématique.* 2 vols. Leuven: Peeters, 1973.
——. *II: Morphologie syntagmatique, syntaxe.* 2 vols. Leuven: Peeters, 1983.

The purpose of this little book is thus quite modest. It is not a scientific grammar, but a pedagogical complement to a standard grammar or an abbreviated review for those who have once controlled the morphology and syntax of Sahidic Coptic, but permitted their control to slip.

There are a number of people who have assisted with the formation of this aide. Professor Harold W. Attridge of Yale University was kind enough to go through it and make a number of helpful suggestions. I want to thank Harry both for the acumen of his mind and the generosity of his spirit. Professor Bentley Layton, also at Yale University, was kind enough to answer my questions promptly. I want to thank him both for his publications and his generosity. Students at Notre Dame have made numerous suggestions for its improvement. I am indebted to them for their comments. They have found this little book useful and encouraged me to give it broader circulation. I hope that this venue will provide assistance to students elsewhere.

Gregory E. Sterling
University of Notre Dame

TABLE OF CONTENTS

THE ALPHABET

Letter[1]	Name[2]	Transliteration	Pronounciation[3]
ⲁ	ⲁⲗϥⲁ	a	h*a*t
ⲃ	ⲃⲏⲧⲁ	b	*b*etter
ⲅ	ⲅⲁⲙⲙⲁ	g	*g*ood
ⲇ	ⲇⲁⲗⲇⲁ	d	*d*og
ⲉ	ⲉⲓ	e	s*e*t
ⲍ	ⲍⲏⲧⲁ	z	*z*oo
ⲏ	ϩⲏⲧⲁ	ē	l*a*te
ⲑ	ⲑⲏⲧⲁ	th	ⲧ + ϩ
ⲓ (ⲉⲓ)	ⲓⲱⲧⲁ	i (ei)	mach*i*ne
ⲕ	ⲕⲁⲡⲡⲁ	k	*k*ind
ⲗ	ⲗⲁⲩⲇⲁ	l	*l*amb
ⲙ	ⲙⲏ	m	*m*ore
ⲛ	ⲛⲉ	n	*n*one
ⲝ	ⲝⲓ	ks	ⲕ + ⲥ
ⲟ	ⲟⲩ	o	d*o*g
ⲡ	ⲡⲓ	p	*p*ot
ⲣ	ⲣⲱ	r	*r*aw
ⲥ	ⲥⲏⲙⲙⲁ	s	*s*ee
ⲧ	ⲧⲁⲩ	t	*t*op
ⲩ (ⲟⲩ)	ϩⲉ	u (ou)	f*oo*d
ⲫ	ⲫⲓ	ph	ⲡ + ϩ
ⲭ	ⲭⲓ	kh	ⲕ + ϩ
ⲯ	ⲯⲓ	ps	ⲡ + ⲥ
ⲱ	ⲱ	ō	l*o*pe
ϣ	ϣⲁⲓ	š	*sh*ell
ϥ	ϥⲁⲓ	f	*f*air
ϩ	ϩⲟⲣⲓ	h	*h*ope
ϫ	ϫⲁⲛϫⲓⲁ	j, ğ	*j*udge
ϭ	ϭⲓⲙⲁ	č, c	*ch*urch
ϯ	ϯ	ti	ⲧ + ⲓ

[1] The alphabet consists of thirty letters: the twenty-four letters of the Greek alphabet and six letters from the Egyptian Demotic script that have been modified to resemble the style of Greek uncial script. The Greek characters come first; the Demotic characters are the final six characters.

[2] These are the traditional names listed in W. E. Crum, *A Coptic Dictionary* (Oxford: Clarendon, 1939).

[3] The pronounciations are conventional.

NUMBERS

Introductory Notes

1. Coptic uses the letters of the alphabet to mark numbers unless they are part of a literary text in which case they are written out. When the alphabet is used, the letter normally has a superlinear stroke over it, e.g., ⲓ̄ⲁ̄ (=11).
2. Grammatical gender is expressed for numbers one through ten; numbers twenty and thirty; and numbers above ten that end in the digits one, two, eight, or nine, e.g., twenty-one is ϫⲟⲩⲧⲟⲩⲉ (m.) and ϫⲟⲩⲧⲟⲩⲉⲓ (f.).
3. Compound numbers are usually formed by combining the higher prefixal form with the appropriate lower suffixal form, e.g., the prefixal form of ten (ⲙⲛ̄ⲧ—) plus the suffixal form of two (—ⲥⲛⲟⲟⲩⲥ) makes twelve (ⲙⲛ̄ⲧⲥⲛⲟⲟⲩⲥ). In some cases, the two units are connected by the adjectival marker ⲛ̄, e.g., ⲥⲉ ⲛ̄ ϣⲉ (600). In a few cases, a prefixal form of the smaller unit is combined with the larger unit, e.g., ⲥⲉⲩϣⲉ (600).
4. When the numbers are written out, they move from the highest to the lowest unit, e.g., ϩⲙⲉⲛⲉⲧⲁϥⲧⲉ ⲛ̄ ⲣⲟⲙⲡⲉ ("eighty-four years") or ⲙⲛ̄ⲧⲥⲛⲟⲟⲩⲥ ⲛ̄ ϣⲉ ⲙⲛ̄ ⲥⲉ ("twelve hundred and sixty").
5. Numbers are combined with nouns in different ways. The number one precedes the noun it modifies and may or may not be linked with a ⲛ̄. The number two follows the noun that it modifies in apposition without a connecting ⲛ̄. The numbers three and higher precede the noun that they modify and are linked with a ⲛ̄.

Sym.	Num.	Independent Forms		Suffixal Forms		Prefixal Forms
		Masculine	Feminine	Masculine	Feminine	
ⲁ̄	1	ⲟⲩⲁ	ⲟⲩⲉⲓ	—ⲟⲩⲉ	—ⲟⲩⲉⲓ	
ⲃ̄	2	ⲥⲛⲁⲩ	ⲥⲛ̄ⲧⲉ	—ⲥⲛⲟⲟⲩⲥ	—ⲥⲛⲟⲟⲩⲥⲉ	
ⲅ̄	3	ϣⲟⲙⲛ̄ⲧ	ϣⲟⲙⲧⲉ	—ϣⲟⲙⲧⲉ		ϣⲙ̄ⲧ—
						ϣⲙⲛ̄ⲧ—
ⲇ̄	4	ϥⲧⲟⲟⲩ	ϥⲧⲟ, ϥⲧⲟⲉ	—ⲁϥⲧⲉ		ϥⲧⲟⲩ—
ⲉ̄	5	ϯⲟⲩ	ϯ, ϯⲉ	—ⲧⲏ		
ⲋ̄	6	ⲥⲟⲟⲩ	ⲥⲟ, ⲥⲟⲉ	—ⲁⲥⲉ		ⲥⲉⲩ—
ⲍ̄	7	ⲥⲁϣϥ̄	ⲥⲁϣϥⲉ	—ⲥⲁϣϥⲉ		
ⲏ̄	8	ϣⲙⲟⲩⲛ	ϣⲙⲟⲩⲛⲉ	—ϣⲙⲏⲛ	—ϣⲙⲏⲛⲉ	
ⲑ̄	9	ⲯⲓⲥ	ⲯⲓⲧⲉ	—ⲯⲓⲥ	—ⲯⲓⲧⲉ	
ⲓ̄	10	ⲙⲏⲧ	ⲙⲏⲧⲉ			ⲙⲛ̄ⲧ—
ⲓ̄ⲁ̄	11	ⲙⲛ̄ⲧⲟⲩⲉ	ⲙⲛ̄ⲧⲟⲩⲉⲓ			
ⲓ̄ⲃ̄	12	ⲙⲛ̄ⲧⲥⲛⲟⲟⲩⲥ	ⲙⲛ̄ⲧⲥⲛⲟⲟⲩⲥ(ⲉ)			
ⲓ̄ⲅ̄	13	ⲙⲛ̄ⲧϣⲟⲙⲧⲉ				
ⲓ̄ⲇ̄	14	ⲙⲛ̄ⲧⲁϥⲧⲉ				

NUMBERS

Sym.	Num.	Independent Forms		Suffixal Forms		Prefixal Forms
		Masculine	Feminine	Masculine	Feminine	
ⲓ̅ⲉ̅	15	ⲙⲛ̄ⲧⲏ				
ⲓ̅ⲋ̅	16	ⲙⲛ̄ⲧⲁⲥⲉ				
ⲓ̅ⲍ̅	17	ⲙⲛ̄ⲧⲥⲁϣϥ(ⲉ)				
ⲓ̅ⲯ̅	18	ⲙⲛ̄ⲧϣⲙⲏⲛ	ⲙⲛ̄ⲧϣⲙⲏⲛⲉ			
ⲓ̅ϣ̅	19	ⲙⲛ̄ⲧⲯⲓⲥ	ⲙⲛ̄ⲧⲯⲓⲧⲉ			
ⲕ̅	20	ϫⲟⲩⲱⲧ	ϫⲟⲩⲱⲧⲉ			ϫⲟⲩⲧ—
ⲕ̅ⲁ̅	21	ϫⲟⲩⲧⲟⲩⲉ	ϫⲟⲩⲧⲟⲩⲉⲓ			
ⲕ̅ⲃ̅	22	ϫⲟⲩⲧⲥⲛⲟⲟⲩⲥ	ϫⲟⲩⲧⲥⲛⲟⲟⲩⲥ(ⲉ)			
ⲕ̅ⲅ̅	23	ϫⲟⲩⲧϣⲟⲙⲧⲉ				
ⲕ̅ⲇ̅	24	ϫⲟⲩⲧⲁϥⲧⲉ				
ⲕ̅ⲉ̅	25	ϫⲟⲩⲧⲏ				
ⲕ̅ⲋ̅	26	ϫⲟⲩⲧⲁⲥⲉ				
ⲕ̅ⲍ̅	27	ϫⲟⲩⲧⲥⲁϣϥ(ⲉ)				
ⲕ̅ⲏ̅	28	ϫⲟⲩⲧϣⲙⲏⲛ	ϫⲟⲩⲧϣⲙⲏⲛⲉ			
ⲕ̅ⲑ̅	29	ϫⲟⲩⲧⲯⲓⲥ	ϫⲟⲩⲧⲯⲓⲧⲉ			
ⲗ̅	30	ⲙⲁⲁⲃ	ⲙⲁⲁⲃⲉ			ⲙⲁⲃ—
ⲙ̅	40	ϩⲙⲉ				ϩⲙⲉ—[4]
ⲛ̅	50	ⲧⲁ(ⲉ)ⲓⲟⲩ				ⲧⲁⲉⲓⲟⲩ—
ⲝ̅	60	ⲥⲉ				ⲥⲉ—[4]
ⲟ̅	70	ϣϥⲉ				ϣϥⲉ—
ⲡ̅	80	ϩⲙⲉⲛⲉ				ϩⲙⲉⲛⲉ—[4]
ϥ̅	90	ⲡⲥⲧⲁⲓⲟⲩ				ⲡⲥⲧⲁⲓⲟⲩ—
ⲣ̅	100	ϣⲉ				
ⲥ̅	200	ϣⲏⲧ				
ⲧ̅	300	ϣⲙⲛ̄ⲧ—ϣⲉ				
ⲩ̅	400	ϥⲧⲟⲩ—ϣⲉ				
ⲫ̅	500	ϯⲟⲩ ϣⲉ				
ⲭ̅	600	ⲥⲉⲩ—ϣⲉ				
ⲯ̅	700	ⲥⲁϣϥ̄ ϣⲉ				
ⲱ̅	800	ϣⲙⲟⲩⲛ ϣⲉ				
ϡ̅	900	ⲯⲓⲥ ϣⲉ				
ⲁ̿	1000	ϣⲟ				
	10,000	ⲧⲃⲁ				

[4] The prefixal forms of the numbers ϩⲙⲉ— (forty), ⲥⲉ— (sixty), and ϩⲙⲉⲛⲉ— (eighty) take a ⲧ before the suffixal forms ⲁϥⲧⲉ (four) and —ⲁⲥⲉ (six), e.g., ϩⲙⲉⲛⲉⲧⲁϥⲧⲉ (eighty-four).

PART ONE

ARTICLES AND PRONOUNS

ARTICLES

Indefinite Articles

	Simple Form		Full Form	
	Singular	Plural	Singular	Plural
M.	___	___	ⲟⲩ—	ϩⲉⲛ—
F.	___	___	ⲟⲩ—	ϩⲉⲛ—

Definite Articles

	Simple Form		Full Form	
	Singular	Plural	Singular	Plural
M.	ⲡ—	ⲛ̄—	ⲡⲉ—	ⲛⲉ—
F.	ⲧ—	ⲛ̄—	ⲧⲉ—	ⲛⲉ—

NOTES:

1. Indefinite article
   a. ⲟⲩ can contract or reduce to —ⲩ— with a prefix to become ⲁⲩ (ⲁ + ⲟⲩ) or ⲉⲩ (ⲉ + ⲟⲩ).
   b. ϩⲉⲛ also appears as ϩⲛ̄.
2. Definite article
   a. ⲛ̄
      1.) May be ⲛ̄ or ⲛ before a vowel.
      2.) Becomes ⲙ̄ before ⲙ and ⲡ.
   b. The full or plene forms of the definite article are typically used:
      1.) Before nouns beginning with two or more consonants or a double consonant, e.g., ⲡⲉⲣ̄ⲣⲟ, ⲧⲉⲥⲃⲱ, ⲡⲉϩⲟⲩⲟ, ⲧⲉϩⲓⲏ, ⲡⲉⲫⲓⲗⲟⲥⲟⲫⲟⲥ, ⲧⲉⲯⲩⲭⲏ.
      2.) Units of time, i.e., ⲧⲉⲣⲟⲙⲡⲉ, ⲡⲉⲟⲩⲟⲉⲓϣ, ⲡⲉϩⲟⲟⲩ.
      EXCEPTION: ⲡⲛⲁⲩ

PRONOUNS

DEMONSTRATIVE PRONOUNS

Affective Demonstrative Pronouns

	Prenominal Form or Article[1]	Absolute Form or Independent Pronoun
m.s.	ⲡⲓ—	ⲡⲏ
f.s.	ϯ—	ⲧⲏ
pl.	ⲛⲓ—	ⲛⲏ

Near Demonstrative Pronouns

	Prenominal Form or Article	Absolute Form or Independent Pronoun
m.s.	ⲡⲉⲓ—	ⲡⲁⲓ
f.s.	ⲧⲉⲓ—	ⲧⲁⲓ
pl.	ⲛⲉⲓ—	ⲛⲁⲓ

Remote Demonstrative Pronouns

	Prenominal Form or Article[2]	Absolute Form or Independent Pronoun[3]
m.s.	ⲡ—... ⲉⲧⲙ̄ⲙⲁⲩ	ⲡⲉⲧⲙ̄ⲙⲁⲩ
f.s.	ⲧ—... ⲉⲧⲙ̄ⲙⲁⲩ	ⲧⲉⲧⲙ̄ⲙⲁⲩ
pl.	ⲛ̄—... ⲉⲧⲙ̄ⲙⲁⲩ	ⲛⲉⲧⲙ̄ⲙⲁⲩ

INDEFINITE PRONOUNS

ⲗⲁⲁⲩ	*anyone, anything; no one, nothing*
ⲟⲩⲁ, ⲟⲩⲉⲓ	*a certain one*
ⲟⲩⲟⲛ	*someone, something; no one, nothing*
ⲛ̄ⲟⲩⲟⲛ, ϩⲉⲛⲟⲩⲟⲛ	*some*
ⲟⲩⲟⲛ ⲛⲓⲙ	*everyone*

[1] Grammars typically classify these forms as pronouns, but sometimes as articles. The forms use the definite article with a pronominal suffix. I have placed them with the pronouns since students will probably encounter them as pronouns in beginning grammars.

[2] This consists of the definite article, a noun, and a relative clause. The whole construction functions as the article form of the remote demonstrative pronoun, "that (noun)."

[3] This substantivized form of a relative clause functions as the remote demonstrative pronoun "that one."

Intensive Pronouns

ⲙⲁⲩⲁⲁ=	*alone, only, self, sole*
ⲙ̄ⲙⲓⲛ ⲙ̄ⲙⲟ=	*possessive or reflective sense*
ϩⲱⲱ=	*also, however, moreover, too*
ϩⲁⲣⲓϩⲁⲣⲟ=	*alone, apart (used appositionally)*

Interrogative Pronouns

ⲁϣ	*what?*
ⲁϣ ⲙ̄ ⲙⲓⲛⲉ	*what sort?*
ⲁϣ ⲛ̄ ϩⲉ	*what sort?*
ⲛⲓⲙ	*who? what?*
ⲟⲩ	*what?*
ⲟⲩ ⲙ̄ ⲙⲓⲛⲉ	*what sort?*
ⲟⲩⲏⲣ	*how much? how many? how great?*

Personal Pronouns

	Proclitic		Absolute or Independent	
	Singular	Plural	Singular	Plural
1	ⲁⲛⲅ̄—	ⲁⲛ—	ⲁⲛⲟⲕ	ⲁⲛⲟⲛ
2m.	ⲛ̄ⲧⲕ̄—	ⲛ̄ⲧⲉⲧⲛ̄—	ⲛ̄ⲧⲟⲕ	ⲛ̄ⲧⲱⲧⲛ̄
2f.	ⲛ̄ⲧⲉ—		ⲛ̄ⲧⲟ	
3m.	____	____	ⲛ̄ⲧⲟϥ	ⲛ̄ⲧⲟⲟⲩ
3f.	____		ⲛ̄ⲧⲟⲥ	

Possessive Pronouns

	Prenominal Possessive Pronouns or Possessive Articles		***Absolute Possessive Pronouns***	
	Masculine		Masculine	
	Singular	Plural	Singular	Plural
1	ⲡⲁ—	ⲡⲉⲛ—	ⲡⲱⲓ	ⲡⲱⲛ
2m.	ⲡⲉⲕ—	ⲡⲉⲧⲛ̄—	ⲡⲱⲕ	ⲡⲱⲧⲛ̄
2f.	ⲡⲟⲩ—		ⲡⲱ	
3m.	ⲡⲉϥ—	ⲡⲉⲩ—	ⲡⲱϥ	ⲡⲱⲟⲩ
3f.	ⲡⲉⲥ—		ⲡⲱⲥ	

	Feminine		Feminine	
	Singular	Plural	Singular	Plural
1	ⲧⲁ—	ⲧⲉⲛ—	ⲧⲱⲓ	ⲧⲱⲛ
2m.	ⲧⲉⲕ—	ⲧⲉⲧⲛ̄—	ⲧⲱⲕ	ⲧⲱⲧⲛ̄
2f.	ⲧⲟⲩ—		ⲧⲱ	
3m.	ⲧⲉϥ—	ⲧⲉⲩ—	ⲧⲱϥ	ⲧⲱⲟⲩ
3f.	ⲧⲉⲥ—		ⲧⲱⲥ	

	Common Plural		Common Plural	
	Singular	Plural	Singular	Plural
1	ⲛⲁ—	ⲛⲉⲛ—	ⲛⲟⲩⲓ	ⲛⲟⲩⲛ
2m.	ⲛⲉⲕ—	ⲛⲉⲧⲛ̄—	ⲛⲟⲩⲕ	ⲛⲟⲩⲧⲛ̄
2f.	ⲛⲟⲩ—		ⲛⲟⲩ	
3m.	ⲛⲉϥ—	ⲛⲉⲩ—	ⲛⲟⲩϥ	ⲛⲟⲩⲟⲩ
3f.	ⲛⲉⲥ—		ⲛⲟⲩⲥ	

Proclitic Possessive Pronouns ("the one[s] or thing[s] belonging to")

Masculine	Feminine	Common Plural
ⲡⲁ—	ⲧⲁ—	ⲛⲁ—

Reciprocal Pronoun

—ⲉⲣⲏⲩ

Relative Converters

Note: Relative pronouns are part of the system of conversion in Coptic. Unlike Greek or Latin that have fully developed declensions of relative pronouns or English that has distinct forms, Coptic uses a system of conversion to create relative clauses out of verbal constructions and non-verbal sentences. The relative is therefore treated as part of the verbal system in the section on conversion. The full paradigms are listed in the section on paradigms.

PART TWO

NOUNS AND ADJECTIVES

NOUNS

Introductory Notes

1. Coptic nouns are masculine or feminine in grammatical gender and singular or plural in number. Many infinitives also serve as masculine nouns.
2. Nouns are typically indeclinable. Differences in grammatical gender and number are signaled by definite or indefinite articles. Definite articles mark distinctions between both gender and number while indefinite articles make a distinction in number alone.
3. Some nouns have distinct forms for both masculine and feminine forms of the same or related noun. In these cases the feminine forms of the nouns alter the vowel pattern (and sometimes the syllabic structure) of their masculine counterparts. The first list below provides some of the most common examples.
4. Some nouns have distinct forms for the plural or are exclusively plural. The distinct plural form is optional; Coptic uses both forms for the plural. The second and third lists below present the majority of these two groups as they appear in Sahidic Coptic; they do not include the nouns whose plural forms are only attested in other dialects, e.g., Bohairic. The lists are based on the entries in Crum, *Coptic Dictionary*. There are often several variations in spelling; the lists below only include the first or possibly the first and second entries in Crum. Students should consult Crum or a major lexicon for fuller lists of forms. There are some observable patterns.
   a. A plural marker may be added to the stem. Some of these are:
      —ⲁⲧⲉ
      —ⲉⲉⲩ
      —ⲉⲉⲩⲉ
      —ⲏⲩⲉ NOTE: The ⲏ is generally a lengthened ⲉ.
      —ⲟⲧⲉ
      —ⲟⲟⲩⲉ NOTE: some Greco-Coptic nouns form the plural in this way, e.g., ⲯⲩⲭⲏ, ⲯⲩⲭⲟⲟⲩⲉ (*soul, souls*)
   b. In other cases the stem changes by doubling the vowel or replacing it e.g., ϣⲃⲏⲣ, ϣⲃⲉⲉⲣ (*companion, companions*). There are other shifts as well.
   c. It is possible to combine these two patterns, e.g., ⲥⲟⲛ, ⲥⲛⲏⲩ (*brother, brothers*).
5. There are a number of compound nouns. The fourth list below offers the most significant of these. Coptic forms compound nouns in at least three ways.
   a. Two nouns may stand in an attributive construction marked by ⲛ̄, e.g., ⲙⲁ ⲛ̄ ϣⲙ̄ϣⲉ, *place of worship* or ⲥⲁ ⲛ̄ ⲏⲣⲡ̄, *seller of wine*. These are common. Students should consult the lexica for these under the second noun.
   b. There are a number of nouns that appear in a construct state. Or these nouns have reduced forms and do not use ⲛ̄. The list below provides examples of these.
   c. Coptic also uses construct participles that are often individually called *participium conjunctivum* (p.c.) to express an enduring attribute of a human or animal. The *participium conjunctivum* is derived from the infinitive. It is vocalized with an ⲁ that replaces the stressed vowel.
   d. There are also some prefixes that students would do well to learn.

6. Coptic contains a large number of Greek nouns. Greek nouns retain their gender as masculine or feminine nouns. Neuter nouns in Greek become masculine in Coptic.
7. The lists below illustrate the patterns in nouns. It is not necessary for students to memorize these lists. It is important to recognize the patterns attested in the lists.

Related Masculine and Feminine Nouns

Masculine	Common Meaning	Feminine	Common Meaning
ⲁⲃⲟⲕ	*crow, raven*	ⲁⲃⲟⲕⲉ	*crow, raven*
ⲃⲓⲣ	*basket*	ⲃⲓⲣⲉ, ⲃⲁⲓⲣⲉ	*basket*
ⲉⲥⲟⲟⲩ	*sheep*	ⲉⲥⲱ	*sheep*
ⲉϭⲱϣ	*Ethiopian*	ⲉϭⲟⲟϣⲉ	*Ethiopian*
ⲕⲉⲕⲉ	*pupil (of eye)*	ⲕⲁⲕⲉ	*pupil (of eye)*
ⲙⲉⲥⲧⲉ	*hated person*	ⲙⲉⲥⲧⲏ	*hated person*
ⲛⲟⲩⲧⲉ	*god*	ⲛⲧⲱⲣⲉ	*god*
ⲣⲙ̄ϩⲉ	*free person*	ⲣⲙ̄ϩⲏ	*free person*
ⲣ̄ⲣⲟ	*king*	ⲣ̄ⲣⲱ	*queen*
ⲥⲟⲛ	*brother*	ⲥⲱⲛⲉ	*sister*
ⲥⲏϭ	*foal*	ⲥⲉⲉϭⲉ	*foal*
ⲟⲩϩⲟⲣ	*dog*	ⲟⲩϩⲱⲣⲉ	*dog*
ϣⲃⲏⲣ	*friend*	ϣⲃⲉⲉⲣⲉ	*friend*
ϣⲟⲙ	*father-in-law son-in-law*	ϣⲱⲙⲉ	*mother-in-law daughter-in-law*
ϣⲙ̄ⲙⲟ	*stranger*	ϣⲙ̄ⲙⲱ	*stranger*
ϣⲏⲣⲉ	*son*	ϣⲉⲉⲣⲉ	*daughter*
ϩⲁⲉ	*end*	ϩⲁⲏ	*end*
ϩⲓⲉⲓⲃ	*lamb*	ϩ(ⲉ)ⲓⲁ(ⲉ)ⲓⲃⲉ	*lamb*
ϩⲗ̄ⲗⲟ	*old man, monk*	ϩⲗ̄ⲗⲱ	*old woman*
ϩⲧⲟ	*horse*	ϩⲧⲱⲣⲉ	*horse*
ϩⲟⲩⲉⲓⲧ	*first*	ϩⲟⲩⲉⲓⲧⲉ	*first*
ϩⲟϥ, ϩⲟⲃ	*snake*	ϩϥⲱ, ϩⲃⲱ	*snake*
ϭⲁⲙⲟⲩⲗ	*camel*	ϭⲁⲙⲁⲩⲗⲉ	*camel*

Nouns with Distinct Plural Forms

Singular		Plural	Common Meaning
Masculine	Feminine		
	ⲁⲃⲱ	ⲁⲃⲟⲟⲩⲉ	*drag net*
ⲁⲃⲱⲕ		ⲁⲃⲟⲟⲕⲉ	*crow, raven*
ⲁⲗⲟⲩ	ⲁⲗⲟⲩ	ⲁⲗⲟⲩⲓ	*youth, maiden*
	ⲁⲗⲱ	ⲁⲗⲟⲟⲩⲉ	*pupil of the eye*
	ⲁⲗⲱ	ⲁⲗⲟⲟⲩⲉ	*snare, trap*
ⲁⲙⲉ		ⲁⲙⲏⲩ, ⲁⲙⲏⲩⲉ	*herder, herdsman*
ⲁⲙⲣⲉ		ⲁⲙⲣⲏⲩ	*baker*
ⲁⲛⲁϣ		ⲁⲛⲁⲩϣ	*oath*
	ⲁⲡⲉ	ⲁⲡⲏⲩⲉ	*head*
ⲁⲡⲟⲧ		ⲁⲡⲏⲧ	*cup*
ⲁϥ		ⲁϥⲟⲩⲓ	*flesh*
ⲁϩⲟ		ⲁϩⲱⲱⲣ	*treasure*
ⲃⲉⲕⲉ		ⲃⲉⲕⲏⲩⲉ, ⲃⲉⲕⲉⲉⲩⲉ	*wage*
ⲃⲁϩⲙⲟⲩ		ⲃⲁϩⲙⲟⲟⲩⲉ	*barbarian people of Nile*
ⲃⲓⲣ	ⲃⲓⲣⲉ, ⲃⲁⲓⲣⲉ	ⲃⲣⲏⲟⲩⲉ	*basket*
ⲃⲁⲣⲱⲧ		ⲃⲁⲣⲁⲧⲉ	*brass, bronze*
ⲃⲁⲣⲱϩ		ⲃⲁⲣⲁϩⲉ, ⲃⲁⲣⲁⲁϩ	*transport animal*
ⲃⲉⲥⲛⲏⲧ		ⲃⲉⲥⲛⲁⲧⲉ	*smith*
	ⲃⲁϣⲟⲣ	ⲃⲁϣⲟⲟⲣ	*fox*
ⲉⲃⲣⲁ		ⲉⲃⲣⲏⲩⲉ	*seed*
ⲉⲃⲟⲧ		ⲉⲃⲁⲧⲉ, ⲉⲃⲉⲧⲉ	*month*
ⲉⲕⲱⲧ		ⲉⲕⲟⲧⲉ	*mason*
	ⲉⲙⲟⲩ	ⲉⲙⲟⲟⲩⲉ	*cat*
ⲉⲣⲏⲧ		ⲉⲣⲁⲧⲉ	*vow, promise*
	ⲉⲩⲱ	ⲉⲩⲟⲟⲩⲉ	*pledge, surety*
	ⲉϣⲱ	ⲉϣⲁⲩ	*sow*
ⲉϩⲉ		ⲉϩⲟⲟⲩ, ⲉϩⲏⲩ	*ox, cow*
ⲉⲓⲱ		ⲉⲟⲟⲩ, ⲉⲱⲟⲩ	*donkey*
ⲉⲓⲃ		ⲉⲓⲉⲃⲏ	*hoof, claw*
ⲉⲓⲉⲣⲟ		ⲉⲓⲣⲱⲟⲩ	*river, great canal*
ⲉⲓⲱⲧ		ⲉⲓⲟⲟⲧⲉ	*father*
ⲉⲓⲱϩⲉ		ⲉⲓⲁϩⲟⲩ	*field*
ⲕⲉⲗⲱⲗ		ⲕⲉⲗⲟⲟⲗⲉ	*pitcher, jar*
ⲕⲣⲟ		ⲕⲣⲱⲟⲩ	*shore, limit*

Singular		Plural	Common Meaning
Masculine	Feminine		
ⲕⲁⲥ		ⲕⲁⲁⲥ	*bone, fruitstone*
ⲗⲉⲗⲟⲩ	ⲗⲉⲗⲟⲩ	ⲗⲉⲗⲁⲩⲉ	*young man or young woman*
ⲗⲁϣⲁⲛⲉ		ⲗⲁϣⲛⲏⲩ	*village magistrate*
ⲙⲟⲩⲓ	ⲙⲟⲩⲓ	ⲙⲱⲟⲩⲓ	*lion*
ⲙⲕⲁϩ		ⲙⲕⲟⲟϩ	*pain, difficulty*
	ⲙⲉⲗⲱⲧ	ⲙ̅ⲉⲗⲁⲧⲉ	*ceiling, canopy*
ⲙ̅ⲗⲁϩ		ⲙⲗⲟⲟϩ	*battle*
ⲙⲁⲛⲉ		ⲙⲁⲛⲏⲩ	*herdsman, pastor*
ⲙⲛ̅ⲧⲣⲉ		ⲙⲛ̅ⲧⲣⲉⲉⲩ	*witness, testimony*
ⲙ̅ⲡⲟ, ⲉⲙⲡⲟ		ⲉⲃⲟⲟⲩⲉ	*dumb person (unable to speak)*
	ⲙⲣⲱ	ⲙⲣⲟⲟⲩⲉ	*harbor*
ⲙⲁⲣϫⲱϫⲉ		ⲙⲁⲣϫⲟⲟϫⲉ	*woman's garment*
ⲙ̅ⲥⲁϩ		ⲙ̅ⲥⲟⲟϩ	*crocodile*
ⲙⲟⲟⲩ		ⲙⲟⲩⲉⲓⲏ, ⲙⲟⲩⲉⲓⲟⲟⲩⲉ	*water*
ⲛⲟⲩⲧⲉ	ⲛ̅ⲧⲱⲣⲉ	ⲉⲛⲧⲏⲣ	*god*
ⲡⲉ		ⲡⲏⲩⲉ	*heaven, sky*
	ⲡⲁϩⲉ	ⲡⲟⲟϩⲉⲩⲉ	*fragment*
ⲣⲟ		ⲣⲱⲟⲩ	*mouth, door*
	ⲣⲙ̅ⲉⲓⲏ	ⲣⲙ̅ⲉⲓⲟⲟⲩⲉ	*tear*
	ⲣⲟⲙⲡⲉ	ⲣⲙ̅ⲡⲟⲟⲩⲉ	*year*
ⲣⲙ̅ϩⲉ	ⲣⲙ̅ϩⲏ	ⲣⲙ̅ϩⲉⲉⲩⲉ	*free person*
ⲣ̅ⲡⲉ		ⲣ̅ⲡⲏⲩⲉ	*temple*
ⲣ̅ⲣⲟ		ⲣ̅ⲣⲱⲟⲩ	*king*
	ⲣ̅ⲥⲱ	ⲣ̅ⲥⲟⲟⲩⲉ	*fold (for animals)*
ⲣⲱⲧ		ⲣⲁⲧⲉ	*a growth*
	ⲥⲃⲱ	ⲥⲃⲟⲟⲩⲉ	*teaching*
ⲥⲟⲛ	ⲥⲱⲛⲉ	ⲥⲛⲏⲩ	*brother, sister*
ⲥⲛⲟϥ		ⲥⲛⲱⲱϥ	*blood*
ⲥⲛⲁϩ		ⲥⲛⲟⲟⲩϩ (?)	*bond, fetter*
ⲥⲟⲡ		ⲥⲱⲡ, ⲥⲱⲱⲡ, ⲥⲟⲟⲡ	*occasion, time*
ⲥⲡⲓⲣ		ⲥⲡⲓⲣⲟⲟⲩⲉ	*rib*
ⲥⲟⲧ, ⲥⲟⲟⲧ		ⲥⲁⲁⲧⲉ	*dung, excrement*
ⲥⲟⲧⲉ	ⲥⲟⲧⲉ	ⲥⲟⲟⲧⲉ	*arrow, dart*
ⲥⲓⲟⲩⲣ		ⲥⲓⲟⲩⲣⲉ (?)	*eunuch*

Singular		Plural	Common Meaning
Masculine	Feminine		
	ⲥⲁϣ	ⲥⲏϣⲉ	*stroke, blow*
	ⲥⲱϣⲉ	ⲥⲟⲟϣⲉ	*field, meadow*
	ⲥϩⲓⲙⲉ	ϩⲓⲟⲙⲉ	*woman, wife*
ⲧⲃ̄ⲛⲏ		ⲧⲃ̄ⲛⲟⲟⲩⲉ	*beast, domestic animal*
ⲧⲗⲟⲙ		ⲧⲗⲟⲟⲙ	*furrow*
ϯⲙⲉ		ⲧⲙⲉ	*village*
ⲧⲟⲟⲩ		ⲧⲟⲩⲉⲓⲏ	*mountain, monastery*
ⲧⲉϣⲉ	ⲧⲉϣⲉ	ⲧⲉϣⲉⲉⲩ	*neighbor*
ⲟⲩⲟⲉⲓⲉ		ⲟⲩⲉⲉⲓⲏ, ⲟⲩⲉⲓⲏ	*farmer*
	ⲟⲩⲛⲟⲩ	ⲟⲩⲛⲟⲟⲩⲉ	*hour*
	ⲟⲩϣⲏ	ⲟⲩϣⲟⲟⲩⲉ	*night*
ⲟⲩϩⲟⲣ	ⲟⲩϩⲱⲣⲉ	ⲟⲩϩⲟⲟⲣ	*dog*
ϣⲃⲏⲣ	ϣⲃⲉⲉⲣⲉ	ϣⲃⲉⲉⲣ	*friend*
ϣⲃⲱⲧ, ϣⲃⲟⲧ		ϣⲃⲁⲧⲉ	*rod, staff*
ϣⲟⲙ	ϣⲱⲙⲉ	ϣⲙⲟⲩⲓ	*parent-in law child-in-law*
ϣⲙ̄ⲙⲟ	ϣⲙ̄ⲙⲱ	ϣⲙ̄ⲙⲟⲓ	*stranger*
ϣⲛⲉ		ϣⲛⲏⲩ, ϣⲛⲏⲩⲉ	*net*
ϣⲁⲁⲣ		ϣⲁⲁⲣⲉ	*skin, hide*
ϣⲏⲣⲉ	ϣⲉⲉⲣⲉ	ϣⲣⲏⲩ	*child*
ϣⲱⲥ, ϣⲱⲱⲥ		ϣⲟⲟⲥ, ϣⲱⲱⲥ	*shepherd*
ϣⲟⲧ, ϣⲱⲧ		ϣϣⲱⲧⲉ	*pillow, cushion*
ϣⲱⲧ		ⲉϣⲟⲧⲉ, ⲉϣⲁⲧⲉ	*trader, merchant*
ϣⲧⲉ, ϣⲧⲏ		ϣⲧⲏⲩ	*ship's mast*
ϣⲧⲉⲕⲟ		ϣⲧⲉⲕⲱⲟⲩ	*prison*
ϣⲁⲩ		ϣⲏⲩ	*trunk, stump*
	ϣⲏⲩⲉ	ϣⲟⲟⲩⲉ	*altar*
ϣⲟϣ	ϣⲟϣ	ϣⲟⲟϣ	*antelope*
ϣϫⲉ		ϣϫⲏⲩ	*locust*
ϩⲁⲉ	ϩⲁⲏ	ϩⲁⲉⲩ, ϩⲁⲉⲟⲩ	*last thing, end*
ϩⲓⲉ, ϩⲓⲏ		ϩⲓⲏⲩ	*rudder*
	ϩⲓⲏ	ϩⲓⲟⲟⲩⲉ	*road, way*
ϩⲟⲓ		ϩⲓⲉⲉⲩⲉ	*field*
ϩⲱⲃ		ϩⲃⲏⲩⲉ	*thing*
	ϩⲃⲟⲥ	ϩⲃⲱⲱⲥ	*garment*
	ϩⲃⲥⲱ	ϩⲃⲥⲟⲟⲩⲉ	*garment*

Singular		Plural	Common Meaning
Masculine	Feminine		
ϩⲁⲗ	ϩⲁⲗ	ϩⲗⲟⲩⲓⲉ	*servant, slave*
ϩⲁⲗⲏⲧ		ϩⲁⲗⲁⲧⲉ, ϩⲁⲗⲁⲁⲧⲉ	*bird*
ϩⲁⲙ		ϩⲙⲏⲩ, ϩⲙⲉⲩ	*craftsman*
ϩⲟⲉⲓⲙ		ϩⲏⲙⲉ, ϩⲓⲙⲏ	*wave*
ϩⲁⲙϣⲉ		ϩⲁⲙϣⲏⲩⲉ, ϩⲁⲙϣⲟⲟⲩⲉ	*carpenter*
ϩⲗ̄ⲗⲟ	ϩⲗ̄ⲗⲱ	ϩⲗ̄ⲗⲟⲓ	*old person, monk*
ϩⲟⲉⲓⲙ		ϩⲏⲙⲉ, ϩⲓⲙⲏ	*wave*
	ϩⲣⲉ	ϩⲣⲏⲩⲉ	*food*
ϩⲏⲧ		ϩⲧⲉⲉⲩ	*tip, edge*
ϩⲧⲟ	ϩⲧⲱⲣⲉ	ϩⲧⲱⲱⲣ	*horse*
ϩⲁⲧⲣⲉ		ϩⲁⲧⲣⲉⲉⲩ, ϩⲁⲧⲣⲉⲉⲩⲉ	*twin*
ϩⲟⲩⲣⲓⲧ		ϩⲟⲩⲣⲁⲧⲉ	*watchman*
ϩⲟⲩⲏⲧ		ϩⲟⲩⲁⲧⲉ	*passenger*
ϩⲟⲩⲉⲓⲧ	ϩⲟⲩⲉⲓⲧⲉ	ϩⲟⲩⲁⲧⲉ	*first*
ϩⲟϥ, ϩⲟⲃ	ϩϥⲱ, ϩⲃⲱ	ϩⲃⲟⲩⲓ	*snake*
ϫⲟ		ϫⲱⲟⲩ	*arm-pit*
	ϫⲟⲉ	ⲉϫⲏ	*wall*
ϫⲟⲓ		ⲉϫⲏⲩ	*boat, ship*
ϫⲛⲟⲟⲩ		ϫⲛⲟⲟⲩⲉ	*threshing-floor*
ϫⲛⲁϩ		ϫⲛⲁⲩϩ	*forearm*
ϫⲟⲉⲓⲥ		ϫⲓⲥⲟⲟⲩⲉ	*lord, master*
ϫⲓⲥⲉ		ϫⲓⲥⲓⲉⲉⲩ	*height, top*
ϫⲁϫⲉ	ϫⲁϫⲉ	ϫⲓϫⲉⲉⲩ, ϫⲓϫⲉⲉⲩⲉ	*enemy*
ϭⲁⲗⲉ		ϭⲁⲗⲉⲉⲩ, ϭⲁⲗⲉⲉⲩⲉ	*cripple*
ϭⲗⲱⲧ	ϭⲗⲱⲧ	ϭⲗⲟⲟⲧⲉ (dual)	*kidney*
ϭⲱⲙ		ϭⲟⲟⲙ	*garden, vineyard*
ϭⲙⲉ, ϭⲙⲏ		ϭⲙⲏⲩ	*gardener*
ϭⲁⲙⲟⲩⲗ	ϭⲁⲙⲁⲩⲗⲉ	ϭⲁⲙⲁⲩⲗⲉ, ϭⲁⲙⲟⲩⲗⲉ	*camel*
ϭⲉⲣⲱⲃ		ϭⲉⲣⲟⲟⲃ	*rod, staff*
ϭⲉⲣⲏϭ		ϭⲉⲣⲁϭⲉ	*hunter*
ϭⲣⲟϭ, ϭⲣⲟⲟϭ		ϭⲣⲱⲱϭ, ϭⲣⲟⲟϭ	*seed*

Nouns that are Mainly Plural

Plural	Common Meaning (Singular)
ⲁⲗⲧⲕⲁⲥ	*marrow*
ⲁⲗⲱⲟⲩⲉ	*bunch of grapes*
ⲁⲣⲟⲟⲩⲉ, ⲁⲣⲱⲟⲩ	*burr, thistle*
ⲉⲡⲣⲁ	*vanity*
ⲉⲥⲟⲟⲩ	*sheep*
ⲉⲓⲟⲩⲉ	*water*
ⲕⲉⲕⲟⲩⲗⲉ	*lump, pustule*
ⲕⲉⲗⲗⲉ	*bolt, knee*
ⲗⲟⲩⲃⲟⲓⲉ	*ship (type of Nile ship)*
ⲗⲁϣⲓⲉ	*hypocrite*
ⲗⲟⲩϫ	*secretion in eye*
ⲙⲟϣⲧⲉ	*parts, neighborhood*
ⲡⲁⲙⲡⲉⲓ	*ring*
ⲥⲉⲃⲟⲟⲛ	*support, prop*
ⲥⲁⲣⲁⲕⲱⲧⲉ	*wanderer, vagrant*
ⲥⲣⲛϩ	*eyebrow*
ⲟⲩⲱϭ	*jaw, cheek? entrance, portico*
ϩⲁⲃⲟⲩⲉⲓ, ϩⲁⲃⲓⲟⲩⲓ	*wasp*
ϩⲟⲕⲙⲉⲥ	*palanquin, litter*
ϩⲏⲛⲉ	*spice, incense*
ϩⲟⲉⲓⲛⲉ	*some, certain*
ϩⲣⲟⲩϫⲉⲃ	*pebbles*
ϩⲣⲱϫⲉ	*boundary*
ϩⲁϩ	*many*
ϭⲉⲃϭⲓⲃ	*fragments, shreds*
ϭⲗⲓⲗ	*axe*

Compound Nouns

Construct Nouns

Note: I have provided examples where they appear in Crum, *Coptic Dictionary* or when the compound is common. I have attempted to provide examples for all nouns. In instances where Crum does not provide a clear example, I have created one and marked it with an asterisk. Note that in some examples there is an intervening ⲛ̄.

Noun	Construct	Meaning	Example
ⲁϥ	ⲁϥ—	*meat*	ⲁϥ—ⲣⲓⲣ, *pork*
ⲃⲛⲛⲉ	ⲃⲛ—	*date palm-tree*	ⲃⲛ—ϣⲟⲟⲩⲉ, *dried dates*
ⲃⲟⲛⲧⲉ	ⲃⲛ̄ⲧ—	*gourd, cucumber*	ⲃⲛ̄ⲧ—ⲛ̄—ⲉϭⲗⲟϭ, *pumpkin*
ⲉⲃⲓⲱ	ⲉⲃⲓⲉ—	*honey*	ⲉⲃⲓⲉ—ϩⲟⲟⲩⲧ, *wild honey*
ⲉⲃⲣⲁ	ⲃⲣⲉ—, ⲃⲣⲓ—	*seed*	ⲃⲣⲓ—ⲥⲱϣⲉ, *seed-corn*
ⲉⲗⲟⲟⲗⲉ	ⲉⲗⲉⲗ—	*grape*	ⲉⲗⲉⲗ—ⲕⲏⲙⲉ, *bruise*
ⲏⲣⲡ̄	ⲉⲣⲡ̄—	*wine*	ⲉⲣⲡ—ⲁⲥ, *old wine*
ⲉⲓⲁ	ⲉⲓⲉⲣ—	*eye*	ⲉⲓⲉⲣ—ⲃⲟⲟⲛⲉ, *evil eye*
ⲉⲓⲱ	ⲉⲓⲁ—, ⲓⲁ—	*ass, donkey*	ⲉⲓⲁ—ⲛ̄—ⲧⲟⲟⲩ, *wild ass*
ⲉⲓⲟⲡⲉ	ⲉⲓⲉⲡ—	*craft, art*	ⲉⲓⲉⲡ—ϣⲉ, *woodwork*
ⲉⲓⲱⲧ	ⲉⲓⲧ—	*father*	ⲡⲁⲉⲓⲧ ⲓⲁⲕⲱⲃ, *my father Jacob*
ⲉⲓⲱϩⲉ	ⲉⲓⲱϩ— ⲉⲓⲉϩ—	*field*	ⲉⲓⲉϩ—ⲉⲗⲟⲟⲗⲉ, *vineyard*
ⲕⲉⲗⲉⲃⲓⲛ	ⲕⲉⲗⲁ—	*axe, pickaxe*	ⲕⲉⲗⲁ—ⲉⲕⲱⲧ, *mason's pickaxe*
ⲕⲗ̄ⲗⲉ	ⲕⲉⲗ—	*bolt*	ⲕⲉⲗ—ⲣⲟ, *door bolt**
ⲕⲟⲩⲛϫⲟⲩ	ⲕⲟⲛ—	*vessel*	ⲕⲟⲛ—ⲃⲁⲣⲱⲧ, *bronze vessel**
ⲙⲁⲁϫⲉ	ⲙⲁϫ—	*measure*	ⲙⲁϫ—ϭⲟⲥ, *half measure*
ⲟⲙⲉ	ⲁⲙ—	*clay*	ⲁⲙ—ⲡⲏⲣϣ̄, *red clay*
ⲡⲁϣⲉ	ⲡⲁϣ—	*half*	ⲡⲁϣ—ⲗⲱϩⲙ̄, *half-cooked*
ⲣⲁ	ⲣⲁ—	*state or condition*	ⲣⲁ—ϣⲁ, *rising*
	ⲣⲁ—, ⲣⲉ—	*part or fraction*	ⲣⲉ—ⲙⲏⲧ, *one-tenth*
ⲣⲱⲙⲉ	ⲣⲙ̄(ⲛ̄)—	*man of* (ⲛ̄)	ⲣⲙ̄ⲛ̄—ⲕⲏⲙⲉ, *Egyptian*
ⲣⲱⲙⲉ	ⲣⲉϥ—	*man who* (ⲉϥ...)	ⲣⲉϥ—ϣⲙ̄ϣⲉ, *worshipper*
ⲣⲟⲙⲡⲉ	ⲣⲙ̄ⲡⲉ— ⲣⲙ̄ⲡ—	*year*	ⲣⲙ̄ⲡ—ϣⲓⲣⲉ, *young person*
ⲣⲁⲛ	ⲣⲉⲛ—	*name*	ⲣⲉⲛ—ⲙ̄—ⲙⲏⲧ, *true name*
ⲣⲓⲣ	ⲣⲣ̄—	*swine, pig*	ⲣⲣ̄—ϩⲟⲟⲩⲧ, *wild pig*
ⲥⲟⲛ	ⲥⲛ̄—	*brother*	ⲥⲛ̄—ⲕⲟⲩⲓ, *little brother*
	ⲥⲡ̄—	*year in dating*	ⲥⲡ̄—ϥⲧⲟ, *year four*
ⲥⲟⲡ	ⲥⲡ̄—, ⲥⲉⲡ—	*time, occasion*	ⲛ̄—ⲥⲉⲡ—ⲥⲛⲁⲩ, *two times*
ⲥⲟⲩⲣⲉ	ⲥⲣ̄—	*thorn*	ⲥⲣ̄—ⲃⲛⲛⲉ, *date-palm thorn*
ⲥⲏⲩ	ⲥⲟⲩ—	*time, season*	ⲥⲟⲩ-ⲥⲛⲁⲩ, *second day*
ⲥⲓⲟⲩ	ⲥⲟⲩ—	*star*	ⲥⲟⲩ—ⲛ̄—ϩⲧⲟⲟⲩⲉ, *morning star*
ⲥⲁϣ	ϣⲥ̄—	*stroke, blow*	ϣⲥ̄—ⲛ̄—ⲉⲓϥⲧ̄, *blow of nail*

Noun	Construct	Meaning	Example
ⲥⲟϭⲛ̄	ⲥⲕⲉⲛ—	*ointment*	ⲥⲕⲉⲛ—ⲉ—ⲡⲓⲥⲉ, *cooking grease*
ⲧⲏⲩ	ⲧⲟⲩ—	*wind*	ⲧⲟⲩ—ⲣⲏⲥ, *south wind*
ⲟⲩⲱⲛ	ⲟⲩⲛ̄—	*part (in fractions)*	ⲟⲩⲛ̄—ⲛ̄—ϥⲧⲟⲟⲩ, *a fourth*
ϣⲃⲏⲣ	ϣⲃⲣ̄—	*companion in*	ϣⲃⲣ̄—ⲟⲩⲱⲙ, *eating companion*
ϣⲁⲁⲣ	ϣⲁⲣ—	*skin*	ϣⲁⲣ—ⲃⲁⲁⲙⲡⲉ, *goat skin*
ϣⲏⲣⲉ	ϣⲣ̄—, ϣⲛ̄—	*child*	ϣⲛ̄—ⲙⲁⲁⲩ, *of the same mother*
ϣⲁⲩ	ϣⲟⲩ—	*worthy of*	ϣⲟⲩ—ⲙⲟⲥⲧⲉ, *deserving hatred*
ϩⲉ	ϩ—	*season*	ϩ—ⲃⲱⲱⲛ, *bad season, famine*
ϩⲁⲙ	ϩⲁⲙ—	*craftsman*	ϩⲁⲙϣⲉ, *carpenter*
ϩⲟⲡ	ϩⲁⲡ—	*feast*	ϩⲁⲡ—ⲕⲱⲱⲥ, *funeral*
ϩⲣⲟⲟⲩ	ϩⲣⲟⲩ—	*voice*	ϩⲣⲟⲩ—ⲙ̄—ⲡⲉ, *thunder*
ϩⲟⲟⲩⲧ	ϩⲟⲩⲧ—	*male*	ϩⲟⲩⲧ—ⲥϩⲓⲙⲉ, *male-female*
ϫⲟⲉ	ϫⲉ—, ϫⲓ—	*wall*	ϫⲉ—ⲛ̄—ⲧⲙⲏⲧⲉ, *middle wall*
	ϫⲡ̄—	*hour*	ϫⲡ̄—ϣⲟⲙⲛ̄ⲧ, *the third hour*
ϫⲟⲉⲓⲧ	ϫⲓⲧ—	*olive-tree, olive*	ϫⲓⲧ—ⲛⲟⲩⲧⲙ̄, *sweet olive*
ϭⲟⲥ	ϭⲓⲥ—	*half*	ϭⲓⲥ—ⲟⲩⲛⲟⲩ, *half an hour*

Construct Participles

(The *Participium conjunctivum*)

Infinitive	Meaning	p.c.	Example
ⲃⲟⲗⲃⲗ̄	*to dig*	ⲃⲁⲗⲃⲗ̄—	ⲃⲁⲗⲃⲗ̄—ⲕⲱⲱⲥ, *wizards*
ⲙⲉ	*to love*	ⲙⲁⲓ—	ⲙⲁⲓ—ⲛⲟⲩⲧⲉ, *devout*
ⲙⲓⲥⲉ	*to bear, give birth*	ⲙⲁⲥ—	ⲙⲁⲥ—ⲡⲟⲣⲕ, *mule*
ⲙⲟⲟⲛⲉ	*to tend, feed*	ⲙⲁⲛⲉ—, ⲙⲁⲛ—	ⲙⲁⲛ—ⲉⲥⲟⲟⲩ, *shepherd*
ⲙⲟⲥⲧⲉ	*to hate*	ⲙⲁⲥⲧ—	ⲙⲁⲥⲧ-ⲣⲱⲙⲉ, *misanthropist*
ⲙⲟⲩϣⲧ	*to examine*	ⲙⲁϣⲧ̄—	ⲙⲁϣⲧ̄—ϩⲏⲧ, *heart examiner*
ⲥⲱ	*to drink*	ⲥⲁⲩ—	ⲥⲁⲩ—ⲏⲣⲡ̄, *wine-drinker*
ⲥⲱⲣ	*to scatter*	ⲥⲁⲣ—	ⲥⲁⲣ—ⲙⲟⲟⲩ, *water-distributer*
ⲟⲩⲱⲙ	*to eat*	ⲟⲩⲁⲙ—	ⲟⲩⲁⲙ—ⲣⲱⲙⲉ, *man-eater*
ⲡⲱϫϭ	*to beat flat*	ⲡⲁϫⲕ—, ⲡⲁϫ—	ⲡⲁϫ—ⲟⲩⲉⲣⲏⲧⲉ, *flat-footed*
ϥⲓ	*to carry*	ϥⲁⲓ—	ϥⲁⲓ—ⲛⲁϩⲃ, *beast of burden*
ϩⲗⲟϭ	*be sweet*	ϩⲁⲗϭ—	ϩⲁⲗϭ—ϣⲁϫⲉ, *eloquent*
ϫⲓⲥⲉ	*become high*	ϫⲁⲥⲓ—	ϫⲁⲥⲓ—ϩⲏⲧ, *arrogant*

Prefixes

Prefix	Function	Example
ⲁⲛ—	*great one*, used with numbers	ⲁⲛ—ⲙⲏⲧ, *ruler of ten*
ⲁⲛ—	prefix in collective numerals	ⲁⲛ—ϣⲟ, *group of 1000*
ⲗⲁ—	+ noun=adj., possessing	ⲟⲩⲗⲁ—ϥⲱⲓ, *hairy*
ⲙⲛ̄ⲧ—	abstract	ⲙⲛ̄ⲧ—ⲁⲧⲧⲁⲕⲟ, *imperishable*
ϭⲓⲛ—	act of, manner of	ϭⲓⲛ—ⲛⲁⲩ, *seeing*

ADJECTIVES

Introductory Notes

1. It is debatable whether adjectives exist as a distinct form or whether genderless nouns in attributive constructions function like adjectives. We will use the category adjective, although we caution students that this is a pedagogical strategy more than a grammatical judgment.
2. Adjectives or nouns in attributive constructions that function like adjectives are typically linked by ⲛ̄. There are three possible constructions. The standard attributive construction is definite article and noun + ⲛ̄ + anarthrous adjective, e.g., ⲡϫⲱⲱⲙⲉ ⲛ̄ ϩⲏⲡ (*the hidden book*). The order of the noun and adjective can be reversed in an inverted attributive construction: definite article and adjective + ⲛ̄ + anarthrous noun, e.g., ⲡϩⲏⲡ ⲛ̄ ϫⲱⲱⲙⲉ (*the hidden book*). Finally, in a few cases there are adjectives that follow the noun and do not use ⲛ̄.
3. Some adjectives have relatively fixed positions in relation to the noun: some precede the noun while others follow the noun. Some adjectives do not have fixed positions and may stand either before or after the noun. See the lists below.
4. There are a number of Greek adjectives in Coptic. Most of these come from the two ending adjectives of the second declension, the —ος/ —ον pattern, and appear in the nominative singular form, e.g., ⲇⲓⲕⲁⲓⲟⲥ/ⲇⲓⲕⲁⲓⲟⲛ (*righteous, just*).
5. There are several alternative constructions that have the same function as an adjective:
   a. A noun construction in which the second noun modifies the first, i.e., noun + ⲛ̄ + noun such as ⲟⲩⲙⲁ ⲛ̄ ϫⲁⲉⲓⲉ (*a desert place*) or ⲡⲟⲉⲓⲕ ⲙ̄ ⲙⲉ (*the true bread*). Some of these are so common that they may be thought of as compound expressions, e.g., ⲙⲁ ⲙ̄ ⲙⲟⲟϣⲉ (*a path*, literally a place of walking).
   b. A relative clause, e.g., ⲡⲉⲡ̅ⲛ̅ⲁ̅ ⲉⲧⲟⲩⲁⲁⲃ (*the Holy Spirit*).
   c. When the antecedent is indefinite, the circumstantial clause is used instead of the relative, e.g., ⲟⲩⲡ̅ⲛ̅ⲁ̅ ⲉϥⲟⲩⲁⲁⲃ (*a holy spirit*).
6. When a word in Coptic takes a pronominal suffix, the lexical form uses ⸗ to indicate that this is the prepronominal form, e.g., ⲧⲏⲣ⸗ (*all, whole of*).

Adjectives before a Noun

ⲕⲟⲩⲓ	*small*
ⲙⲉⲣⲓⲧ	*beloved*
ⲛⲟϭ	*great*
ϣⲏⲙ	*small*
ϣⲟⲣⲡ̄	*first*
ϩⲁⲉ	*last*

Adjectives after a Noun without ⲛ̄

ⲁⲥ	*old*
ⲕⲟⲩⲓ	*small*
ⲛⲟϭ	*great*
ⲟⲩⲱⲃϣ̄	*white*
ⲟⲩⲱⲧ	*single*
ϣⲏⲙ	*small*

Special Adjectives

ⲛⲓⲙ	*each, every*
ⲧⲏⲣ=	*all, the whole of*

Inflected Predicate Adjectives

ⲛⲁⲁ— ⲛⲁⲁ=	*great*
ⲛⲁⲛⲟⲩ— ⲛⲁⲛⲟⲩ=	*good*
ⲛⲁⲓⲁⲧ=	*blessed*
ⲛⲉⲥⲉ— ⲛⲉⲥⲱ=	*beautiful*
ⲛⲉⲥⲃⲱⲱ=	*wise*
ⲛⲁϣⲉ— ⲛⲁϣⲱ=	*numerous*
ⲛⲁϩⲗⲱϭ=	*pleasant*
ⲛⲉϭⲱ=	*ugly*

Adjectival Prefixes

ⲁⲧ—	Negative prefix
ⲁⲧⲉ—	*many, various*

PART THREE

PREPOSITIONS AND ADVERBS

PREPOSITIONS

Introductory Notes

1. Prepositions must stand in a larger construction since they are dependent not independent units. They accordingly have two forms: the prenominal (the form before a noun) and the prepronominal (the form with a pronominal suffix marked with a = in the lexical form).
2. The pronominal suffixes on the latter are relatively uniform, although the preposition itself experiences shifts.
3. The easiest way to learn the pronominal suffixes is to learn them with the final vowel of the prepronominal form of the preposition.

Pronominal Suffixes

	Singular	Plural
1	—ⲓ	—ⲛ̄
2m	—ⲕ	—ⲧⲛ̄
2f	—	
3m	—ϥ	—ⲟⲩ
3f	—ⲥ	

NOTE: All plural forms are common for masculine and feminine.

Patterns

Final ⲁ=

	Singular	Plural
1	ⲛⲙ̄ⲙⲁⲓ	ⲛⲙ̄ⲙⲁⲛ
2m	ⲛⲙ̄ⲙⲁⲕ	ⲛⲙ̄ⲙⲏⲧⲛ̄
2f	ⲛⲙ̄ⲙⲉ	
3m	ⲛⲙ̄ⲙⲁϥ	ⲛⲙ̄ⲙⲁⲩ
3f	ⲛⲙ̄ⲙⲁⲥ	

Final ⲏ=

	Singular	Plural
1	ⲟⲩⲃⲏⲓ	ⲟⲩⲃⲏⲛ
2m	ⲟⲩⲃⲏⲕ	ⲟⲩⲃⲉ—ⲧⲏⲩⲧⲛ̄
2f	[ⲟⲩⲃⲏⲧⲉ]	
3m	ⲟⲩⲃⲏϥ	ⲟⲩⲃⲏⲩ
3f	ⲟⲩⲃⲏⲥ	

Final ⲟ=

	Singular	Plural
1	ⲉⲣⲟⲓ	ⲉⲣⲟⲛ
2m	ⲉⲣⲟⲕ	ⲉⲣⲱⲧⲛ̄
2f	ⲉⲣⲟ	
3m	ⲉⲣⲟϥ	ⲉⲣⲟⲟⲩ
3f	ⲉⲣⲟⲥ	

Final ⲱ=

	Singular	Plural
1	ⲉϫⲱⲓ	ⲉϫⲱⲛ
2m	ⲉϫⲱⲕ	ⲉϫⲱⲧⲛ̄
2f	ⲉϫⲱ	
3m	ⲉϫⲱϥ	ⲉϫⲱⲟⲩ
3f	ⲉϫⲱⲥ	

Final ⲧ=

	Singular	Plural
1	ⲛ̄ϩⲏⲧ	ⲛ̄ϩⲏⲧⲛ̄
2m	ⲛ̄ϩⲏⲧⲕ̄	ⲛ̄ϩⲏⲧ—ⲧⲏⲩⲧⲛ̄
2f	ⲛ̄ϩⲏⲧⲉ	
3m	ⲛ̄ϩⲏⲧϥ̄	ⲛ̄ϩⲏⲧⲟⲩ
3f	ⲛ̄ϩⲏⲧⲥ̄	

Common Prepositions in These Patterns

Final ⲁ=

Prenominal Form	Prepronominal Form	Common Meaning(s)
ⲙⲛ̄—	ⲛ̄ⲙ̄ⲙⲁ=	*with, together with*
ⲛ̄—	ⲛⲁ=	*to*
ⲛⲁϩⲣⲛ̄—	ⲛⲁϩⲣⲁ=	*in the presence of, before*

Final ⲏ=

Prenominal Form	Prepronominal Form	Common Meaning(s)
ⲟⲩⲃⲉ—	ⲟⲩⲃⲏ=	*against, opposite*
ϩⲁϩⲧⲛ̄—	ϩⲁϩⲧⲏ=	*near, with, besides*

Final ⲟ=

Prenominal Form	Prepronominal Form	Common Meaning(s)
ⲉ—	ⲉⲣⲟ=	*to*
ⲛ̄—	ⲙ̄ⲙⲟ=	*in*
ϣⲁ—	ϣⲁⲣⲟ=	*to, up to*
ϩⲁ—	ϩⲁⲣⲟ=	*under*

Final ⲱ=

Prenominal Form	Prepronominal Form	Common Meaning(s)
ⲉⲣⲛ̄—	ⲉⲣⲱ=	*to the entrance of*
ⲉϫⲛ̄—	ⲉϫⲱ=	*onto, on*
ⲛⲙ̄ⲙ̄ⲥⲁ—	ⲛⲙ̄ⲙ̄ⲥⲱ=	*after*
ⲛ̄ⲥⲁ—	ⲛ̄ⲥⲱ=	*behind, in back of*
ϩⲓ—	ϩⲓⲱ(ⲱ)=	*on, upon*
ϩⲓⲣⲛ̄—	ϩⲓⲣⲱ=	*at the entrance of*
ϩⲓϫⲛ̄—	ϩⲓϫⲱ=	*on, upon*

Final ⲧ=

Prenominal Form	Prepronominal Form	Common Meaning(s)
ⲉⲧⲃⲉ—	ⲉⲧⲃⲏⲏⲧ=	*about, concerning, because of*
ⲉⲧⲛ̄—	ⲉⲧⲟⲟⲧ=	*to*
ⲛ̄ⲧⲛ̄—	ⲛ̄ⲧⲟⲟⲧ=	*from*
ϩⲓⲧⲛ̄—	ϩⲓⲧⲟⲟⲧ=	*by means of, from with*
ϩⲛ̄—	ⲛ̄ϩⲏⲧ=	*in, within, through*

Prepositions and Compound Prepositions

Introductory Note: Prepositions often appear in compound forms. The following list is based on Crum, *A Coptic Dictionary*. I have given the lexical entry on the far left side. I have subsumed some of the compound prepositional phrases beneath the main entry and indented them. Note that prepositions differ from adverbs by requiring an object. This is generally indicated by the second preposition that sets up the object: ⲉ (ⲉⲣⲟ=) or ⲛ̄ (ⲙ̄ⲙⲟ=). For the sake of space I have only listed the prenominal form of the preposition when it appears in the second position (ⲉ or ⲛ̄). Students should assume that both the prenominal and prepronominal form stand in the second position.

Preposition	Common Meaning
ⲁϫⲛ̄, ⲁϫⲛ̄ⲧ⸗ (ⲉϫⲛ̄, ⲉϫⲛ̄ⲧ⸗)	*without*
ⲃⲱⲗ s.v. ⲃⲟⲗ	(m. noun, *outside*)
ⲡⲃⲟⲗ	*on* or *to the outside of*
ⲙ̄ ⲡⲃⲟⲗ	*on* or *to the outside of*
ⲛ̄ⲃⲗ̄ (ⲛ̄ⲃⲗ̄ⲗⲁ⸗) ⲛ̄—	*without, except for, beyond*
ⲛ̄ ⲥⲁⲃⲏⲗ ⲉ—	*except for, outside of*
ⲥⲁⲃⲟⲗ ⲛ̄—/ⲉ—	*outside of, beyond*
ⲥⲁ ⲛ̄ ⲃⲟⲗ ⲛ̄—/ⲉ—	*outside of, beyond*
ⲛ̄ ⲥⲁ ⲃⲟⲗ ⲛ̄—/ⲉ—	*outside of, beyond*
ⲛ̄ ⲥⲁ ⲛ̄ ⲃⲟⲗ ⲛ̄—/ⲉ—	*outside of, beyond*
ϣⲁⲃⲟⲗ ⲛ̄—	*to the outside of*
ϩⲁⲃⲟⲗ ⲛ̄—	*from, away from*
ϩⲓⲃⲟⲗ ⲛ̄—	*outside of, beyond*
ⲉ (ⲉⲣⲟ⸗)	*to, for, at, in*
ⲉⲃⲟⲗ ⲉ—	*out to, away to*
ⲉⲥⲏⲧ	(m. noun, *ground, bottom*)
ⲉⲡⲉⲥⲏⲧ ⲉ—	*down to, down into*
ⲙ̄ ⲡⲉⲥⲏⲧ ⲛ̄—	*below*
ⲥⲁ—ⲡⲉⲥⲏⲧ ⲛ̄—	*below*
ϩⲁ ⲡⲉⲥⲏⲧ ⲛ̄—	*under*
ⲉⲧⲃⲉ (ⲉⲧⲃⲏⲏⲧ⸗)	*because of, on account of*
ⲕⲱⲧⲉ	(m. noun, *circuit*)
ⲙ̄ ⲕⲱⲧⲉ ⲛ̄—	*around, about, concerning*
ϩⲙ̄ ⲕⲱⲧⲉ ⲛ̄—	*around, about, concerning*
ⲙⲁ	(m. noun, *place*)
ⲉ ⲡⲙⲁ ⲛ̄—	*to, about, in place of*
ⲉ ⲡⲙⲁ ⲛ̄—	*to, regarding, in place of*
ϩⲁ ⲡⲙⲁ ⲛ̄—	*as regards*
ⲙⲛ̄ (ⲛⲙ̄ⲙⲁ⸗)	*with*

Preposition	Common Meaning
ⲙⲏⲧⲉ	(f. noun, *middle*)
ⲉ ⲧⲙⲏⲧⲉ	*to, into the midst of*
ⲛ̄ ⲧⲙⲏⲧⲉ ⲛ̄—	*in the midst of, between*
ⲉⲃⲟⲗ ⲛ̄ ⲧⲙⲏⲧⲉ ⲛ̄—	*from the midst of*
ϩⲛ̄ ⲧⲙⲏⲧⲉ ⲛ̄—	*in the midst of, between*
ⲉⲃⲟⲗ ϩⲛ̄ ⲧⲙⲏⲧⲉ ⲛ̄—	*from the midst of*
ϩⲓ ⲧⲙⲏⲧⲉ ⲛ̄—	*in through the midst of*
ⲙ̄ⲧⲟ	(m. noun, *face, presence*)
ⲙ̄ ⲡⲉⲙⲧⲟ ⲉⲃⲟⲗ ⲛ̄—	*in the presence of, before*
ⲙ̄ ⲡ(=) ⲙ̄ⲧⲟ ⲉⲃⲟⲗ	*in the presence of, before*
ⲙⲁϩ, ⲙ̄ⲙⲁϩ	*before*
ⲛ̄ (ⲙ̄ⲙⲟ=)	Direct object marker Partitive relationships
ⲛ̄ (ⲛⲁ=)	*by, in, to, for*
ⲉⲃⲟⲗ ⲛ̄—	*from, out from*
ⲥⲁ ⲃⲟⲗ ⲛ̄—	*from, out from*
ⲡⲉ	(f. noun, *heaven*)
ⲛ̄ ⲧⲡⲉ ⲛ̄—	*above*
ϩⲛ̄ ⲧⲡⲉ ⲛ̄—	*above*
ⲛ̄ ⲥⲁ—ⲧⲡⲉ ⲛ̄—	*above*
ϩⲓ ⲧⲡⲉ ⲛ̄—	*above*
ⲙ̄ ⲡⲉⲧⲡⲉ ⲛ̄—	*above, over*
ϩⲙ̄ ⲡⲉⲧⲡⲉ ⲛ̄—	*above, over*
ⲡⲁϩⲟⲩ	(m. noun, *back*)
ⲉⲡⲁϩⲟⲩ ⲉ—	*back to*
ⲥⲁ-ⲡⲁϩⲟⲩ	*behind, after*
ϩⲓ ⲡⲁϩⲟⲩ ⲙ̄ⲙⲟ=	*behind*
ⲣⲟ	(m. noun, *mouth, gate*)
ⲉⲣⲛ̄ (ⲉⲣⲱ=)	*to the entrance of*
ϩⲁⲣⲛ̄ (ϩⲁⲣⲱ=)	*before*
ϩⲓⲣⲛ̄ (ϩⲓⲣⲱ=)	*at the entrance of, on*
ⲉⲃⲟⲗ ϩⲓⲣⲛ̄ (ϩⲓⲣⲱ=)	*from before*

Preposition	Common Meaning
ⲣⲁⲧ⸗	(m. noun, *foot, lowest part*)
ⲉⲣⲁⲧ⸗	*to, to the foot of*
ϩⲁⲣⲁⲧ⸗	*under*
ϩⲓⲣⲁⲧ⸗	*toward*
ⲥⲁ	(m. noun, *side, part*)
ⲉ ⲡⲥⲁ ⲛ̄—	*to, beyond*
ⲛ̄ⲥⲁ (ⲛ̄ⲥⲱ⸗)	*behind, after*
ⲙⲛ̄ⲛ̄ⲥⲁ (ⲙⲛ̄ⲛ̄ⲥⲱ⸗)	*after (temporal)*
ⲥⲡⲓⲣ	(m. noun, *rib*)
ⲛ̄ ⲥⲁ—ⲥⲡⲓⲣ ⲙ̄ⲙⲟ⸗	*beside*
ϩⲓ ⲥⲁ—ⲥⲡⲓⲣ ⲙ̄ⲙⲟ⸗	*beside*
ⲧⲱⲣⲉ	(f. noun, *handle [hand]*)
ⲉⲧⲛ̄ (ⲉⲧⲟⲟⲧ⸗)	*to, into the hand of*
ⲛ̄ⲧⲛ̄ (ⲛ̄ⲧⲟⲟⲧ⸗)	*from, from the hand of*
ⲉⲃⲟⲗ ⲛ̄ⲧⲛ̄—	*from*
ϩⲁⲧⲛ̄ (ϩⲁⲧⲟⲟⲧ⸗)	*beside, with, near*
ϩⲓⲧⲛ̄ (ϩⲓⲧⲟⲟⲧ⸗)	*by the hand of, through*
ⲉⲃⲟⲗ ϩⲓⲧⲛ̄—	*by the hand of, through*
ⲧⲟⲩⲱ⸗	(noun, *bosom*)
ⲉⲧⲟⲩⲛ̄ (ⲉⲧⲟⲩⲱ⸗)	*at, near, beside*
ϩⲁⲧⲟⲩⲛ̄ (ϩⲁⲧⲟⲩⲱ⸗)	*at, near, beside*
ϩⲓⲧⲟⲩⲛ̄ (ϩⲓⲧⲟⲩⲱ⸗)	*at, near, beside*
ⲟⲩⲃⲉ (ⲟⲩⲃⲏ⸗)	*against, toward, opposite*
ⲟⲩⲧⲉ (ⲟⲩⲧⲱ⸗)	*between, among*
ⲉⲃⲟⲗ ⲟⲩⲧⲉ ⲛ̄—	*from among*
ϩⲣⲁⲓ ⲟⲩⲧⲉ ⲛ̄—	*among*
ⲟⲩⲱϣ	(m. noun, *gap, cleft*)
(ⲛ̄) ⲟⲩⲉϣ ⲛ̄—	*without*
ϣⲁ (ϣⲁⲣⲟ⸗)	*to, up to*

Preposition	Common Meaning
ϣⲉ, ϣⲁ	*by (in oaths)*
ϣⲱⲓ	(m. noun, *what is high*)
ⲙ̄ ⲡϣⲱⲓ ⲉ—	*above*
ⲥⲁ—ⲡϣⲱⲓ ⲛ̄—	*above*
ϣⲱⲣⲡ̄	(verb, *be early*)
ⲛ̄ ϣⲟⲣⲡ̄ ⲛ̄—	*before*
ϩⲁ (ϩⲁⲣⲟ=)	*under*
ⲉⲃⲟⲗ ϩⲁ—	*away from*
ⲉϩⲟⲩⲛ ϩⲁ—	*in beneath*
ⲉϩⲣⲁⲓ ϩⲁ—	*under, up to*
ϩⲉ, ϩⲓⲏ	(f. noun, *manner*)
ⲛ̄ ϩⲉ ⲛ̄—	*like, in the manner of*
ϩⲏ	(f. noun, *front*)
ϩⲁ ⲑⲏ ⲛ̄—	*in front of, before*
ϩⲓ ⲑⲏ ⲛ̄—	*in front of, before*
ϩⲓ (ϩⲓⲱ=, ϩⲓⲱⲱ=)	*on, upon*
ⲉⲃⲟⲗ ϩⲓ—	*away from on, away from at*
ⲉⲡⲉⲥⲏⲧ ϩⲓ—	*down from*
ⲉϩⲟⲩⲛ ϩⲓ—	*in toward*
ⲉϩⲣⲁⲓ ϩⲓ—	*down from*
ϩⲟ	(m. noun, *face*)
ⲉϩⲣⲛ̄ (ⲉϩⲣⲟ=)	*toward, among*
ⲉⲃⲟⲗ ⲉϩⲣⲛ̄—	*out to*
ⲉϩⲟⲩⲛ ⲉϩⲣⲛ̄—	*into, before, at against*
(ⲛ̄)ⲛⲁϩⲣⲛ̄ ((ⲛ̄)ⲛⲁϩⲣⲁ=)	*in the presence of, before*
ϩⲓ ϩⲣⲁ=	*on the surface of, on the face of*
ϩⲛ̄ (ⲛ̄ϩⲏⲧ=)	*in*
ⲉⲃⲟⲗ ϩⲛ̄—	*from in, from within, out of*
ⲉϩⲟⲩⲛ ϩⲛ̄	*into, within*
ⲛ̄ϩⲟⲩⲛ ϩⲛ̄—	*in, within*
ϩⲣⲁⲓ ϩⲛ̄—	*in*

Preposition	Common Meaning
ϩⲟⲩⲛ	(m. noun, *inside*)
ⲉϩⲟⲩⲛ ⲉ—	*to, toward, into*
ⲉϩⲟⲩⲛ ⲉϩⲣⲛ̄—	*into, before, at against*
ⲉϩⲟⲩⲛ ⲉϫⲛ̄—	*in upon*
ⲉϩⲟⲩⲛ ⲛⲁ=	*to, for*
ⲉϩⲟⲩⲛ ⲛⲁϩⲣⲛ̄—	*before*
ⲉϩⲟⲩⲛ ϣⲁ—	*to, toward, into*
ⲉϩⲟⲩⲛ ϩⲁ—	*in under*
ⲥⲁ—ϩⲟⲩⲛ ⲉ—/ⲛ̄—	*inside, within*
ϣⲁ ϩⲟⲩⲛ ⲉ—	*until*
ϩⲓ ϩⲟⲩⲛ ⲛ̄—	*from within*
ϩⲣⲁⲓ	(m. noun, *upper part*)
ⲉϩⲣⲁⲓ ⲉ—	*up to*
ⲉϩⲣⲁⲓ ⲉϫⲛ̄—	*up onto*
ⲉϩⲣⲁⲓ ⲉϩⲣⲛ̄—	*up into, down into*
ⲉϩⲣⲁⲓ ⲟⲩⲃⲉ—	*up against, down against*
ⲉϩⲣⲁⲓ ϣⲁ—	*up to*
ⲉϩⲣⲁⲓ ϩⲁ—	*up beneath*
ⲉϩⲣⲁⲓ ϩⲓ—	*up on, down on*
ⲉϩⲣⲁⲓ ϩⲛ̄—	*in*
ϣⲁ ϩⲣⲁⲓ ⲉ—	*up to, down to*
ϩⲣⲁⲓ	(m. noun, *lower part*)
ⲉϩⲣⲁⲓ ⲉ—	*down to*
ⲉϩⲣⲁⲓ ⲉϫⲛ̄—	*down upon*
ⲉϩⲣⲁⲓ ϩⲁ—	*under*
ⲉϩⲣⲁⲓ ϩⲛ̄—	*in*
ϣⲁ ϩⲣⲁⲓ ⲉ—	*down to*
ϩⲏⲧ	(m. noun, *heart*)
ϩⲁ(ϩ)ⲧⲛ̄ (ϩⲁ(ϩ)ⲧⲏ=)	*with, near, beside*
ϫⲓⲛ, ϫⲛ̄, ϫⲉⲛ, ⲕⲛ̄, ϭⲛ̄, ϣⲉⲛ	*from, since, starting from*
ϫⲓⲛ ⲉ—	*from, since*
ϫⲓⲛ ⲛ̄—	*from, since*
ϫⲓⲛ ϩⲛ̄—	*from, since*
ϫⲓⲛ ___ ⲉ/ϣⲁ/ϣⲁⲣⲁⲓ ⲉ— ___	*from* ___ *to* ___

Preposition	Common Meaning
ϫⲓⲛ ___ ⲉⲃⲟⲗ/ⲉϩⲣⲁⲓ	*from ___ onward*
ⲉϫⲓⲛ—	*from*
ⲛ̄ϫⲓⲛ—	*from*
ϩⲁϫⲓⲛ—	*from*
ϩⲓϫⲓⲛ—	*from*
ϫⲱ	(m. noun, *head*)
ⲉϫⲛ̄ (ⲉϫⲱ⸗)	*onto, on*
ⲉⲃⲟⲗ ⲉϫⲛ̄—	*out upon*
ⲉϩⲟⲩⲛ ⲉϫⲛ̄—	*into*
ⲉϩⲣⲁⲓ ⲉϫⲛ̄—	*up upon*
ⲉϩⲣⲁⲓ ⲉϫⲛ̄—	*down upon*
ϩⲁϫⲛ̄ (ϩⲁϫⲱ⸗)	*before, in front of*
ϩⲓϫⲛ̄ (ϩⲓϫⲱ⸗)	*on, upon*
ⲉⲃⲟⲗ ϩⲓϫⲛ̄—	*from upon*
ϩⲣⲁⲓ (ⲛ̄) ϩⲓϫⲛ̄—	*upon*

ADVERBS

Introductory Notes

1. Adverbs and prepositions constitute a large number of words or phrases that modify a verb or a verbal unit.
2. Adverbs are either single words or prepositional phrases that are lexically frozen.
3. Simple adverbs are single words, e.g., ⲗⲁⲁⲩ (*at all*) or the interrogative adverb ⲧⲱⲛ (*where*). These are listed in the left hand column. The meanings are listed to the right.
4. Compound adverbs have the structure of a prepositional phrase. They differ from prepositional phrases in two ways. First, the meaning of the phrase is fixed and can not always be understood by combining the meanings of the discrete units. Second, adverbial phrases stand alone; they are not linked to a following noun. As with the prepositions above, I have listed the basic form from which the compound adverbial expressions below it.
5. The following list presents common adverbs and examples of how combinations occur. It is based on on Crum, *A Coptic Dictionary*. The list is not exhaustive. In cases where two identical forms in Coptic are derived from different roots, I have listed the forms separately. I have followed the basic order of the compound phrases as they are listed in Crum.
6. Beginning students do not need to memorize the list below. It is important to know the key nouns, prepositions, and how they form combinations.
7. For the sake of clarity I have organized the adverbs into six basic categories: adverbs of degree or measure, interrogative adverbs, adverbs of manner, spatial adverbs, temporal adverbs, and adverbs that do not easily fit into one of these categories. The headings are listed alphabetically as are the adverbs within each category.

Adverbs of Degree or Measure

ⲕⲟⲩⲓ	(noun or adj., *young, little*)
ⲛ̄ ⲟⲩⲕⲟⲩⲓ	*a little*
ϩⲁⲧⲛ̄ ⲟⲩⲕⲟⲩⲓ	*almost*
ⲛ̄ ⲕⲟⲩⲓ ⲕⲟⲩⲓ	*little by little*
ⲗⲁⲁⲩ	(indef. pronoun, *anyone/thing*)
(ⲛ̄) ⲗⲁⲁⲩ	*at all*
ⲙⲁⲧⲉ	(m. noun, *success*)
ⲉⲙⲁⲧⲉ	*greatly, very much*
ⲙ̄ⲙⲁⲧⲉ	*greatly, very much*

ⲙⲁⲧⲉ *(continued)*

ⲙ̄ⲙⲁⲧⲉ	*only*

ϩⲟⲩⲟ	(m. noun, *greater part*)
ⲉ ⲡⲉϩⲟⲩⲟ	*greatly, very*
ⲛ̄ ϩⲟⲩⲟ	*greatly, very*
ⲛ̄ ϩⲟⲩⲟ ⲉ	*more than*
ⲉ ϩⲟⲩⲟ	*rather*

Interrogative Adverbs

ⲛⲁⲩ	(m. noun, *hour*)
ⲧⲛ̄ⲛⲁⲩ (ⲧⲛⲁⲩ)	*when?*
ⲧⲱⲛ	*where?*
ⲉ ⲧⲱⲛ	*to where (whither)?*
ⲛ̄ ⲧⲱⲛ	*where?*
ⲉⲃⲟⲗ ⲧⲱⲛ	*from where (whence)?*
ϣⲁ ⲧⲱⲛ	*to where (whither)?*
ϩⲛ̄ ⲧⲱⲛ	*where?*
ϫⲓⲛ ⲧⲱⲛ	*from where (whence)?*
ⲟⲩ	(interrog. pronoun, *what, who?*)
ⲉⲧⲃⲉ ⲟⲩ	*why?*
ϩⲉ	(f. noun, *way*)
ⲛ̄ ⲁϣ ⲛ̄ ϩⲉ	*how?*

Adverbs of Manner

Introductory Note: There are two principal ways to form an adverb of manner. They are listed first. Individual adverbs that denote manner are listed after them.

Principal Patterns

ϩⲛ̄ + ⲟⲩ + Noun, e.g.,

ϩⲛ̄ ⲟⲩⲙⲉ	*truly*
ϩⲛ̄ ⲟⲩϫⲱⲕ ⲉⲃⲟⲗ	*completely*

ⲁϫⲛ̄ + Noun, e.g.,

ⲁϫⲛ̄—ϩⲟⲧⲉ	*fearlessly*

Other Examples

ⲁⲣⲏⲩ	*perhaps*
ⲙⲉ	(f. noun, *truth*)
ⲛⲁⲙⲉ	*truly*
ⲙⲉϣⲉ	(verb, *not know*)
ⲙⲉϣⲁⲕ	*perhaps*
ϩⲉ	(f. noun, *manner*)
ⲧⲁⲓ ⲧⲉ ⲑⲉ	*in this way, thus*
ⲛ̅ ⲑⲉ	*in this way, thus*
ⲛ̅ ⲧⲉⲓϩⲉ	*in this way, thus*
ⲛ̅ ⲧⲉⲓϩⲉ ⲧⲏⲣⲥ̅	*so much*
ⲛ̅ ⲧⲉⲓϩⲉ ϩⲁⲡⲗⲱⲥ	*merely thus*
ⲕⲁⲧⲁ ⲑⲉ	*just as, like*
ⲡⲣⲟⲥ ⲑⲉ	*according as*

Spatial Adverbs

Introductory Note: There is a group of spatial adverbs that combine with other adverbs, prepositions, or verbs. When they qualify another adverb or preposition, they precede it; when they qualify a verb, they follow it in much the same way as a preposition does. In such cases they give the verb a specialized meaning. The list below only takes combinations with adverbs and prepositions into consideration. The combinative adverbs are ⲉⲃⲟⲗ, ⲉⲑⲏ, ⲉⲡⲉⲥⲏⲧ, ⲉⲡⲁϩⲟⲩ, ⲉϩⲟⲩⲛ, ⲛ̅ϩⲟⲩⲛ, ϣⲁϩⲟⲩⲛ, ⲉϩⲣⲁⲓ, ⲛ̅ϩⲣⲁⲓ, ϣⲁϩⲣⲁⲓ, and ϩⲣⲁⲓ.

ⲃⲱⲗ s.v. ⲃⲟⲗ	(m. noun, *outside*)
ⲉⲃⲟⲗ	*away, out*
ⲛ̅ ⲃⲟⲗ	*outside*
ⲥⲁⲃⲟⲗ	*outside, without*
ϣⲁⲃⲟⲗ	*outwards, henceforth*
ϩⲁⲃⲟⲗ	*on the outside, from without*
ⲉⲥⲏⲧ	(m. noun, *ground, bottom*)
ⲉⲡⲉⲥⲏⲧ	*downward*
ⲙ̅ ⲡⲉⲥⲏⲧ	*below, down below*
ⲥⲁ—ⲡⲉⲥⲏⲧ	*below, underneath*
ϣⲁ ⲡⲉⲥⲏⲧ	*down to the ground*

ⲉⲥⲏⲧ *(continued)*	
ϩⲁ ⲡⲉⲥⲏⲧ	*underneath*
ϩⲓ ⲡⲉⲥⲏⲧ	*on the ground*
ϫⲓⲛ ⲡⲉⲥⲏⲧ	*from below*
ⲙⲁ	(m. noun, *place*)
ⲉⲩⲙⲁ	*together*
ⲕⲁⲧⲁ ⲙⲁ	*in different places*
ϣⲁ ⲡⲉⲓⲙⲁ	*up to here, so far*
ⲙⲁ ⲛⲓⲙ	*everywhere*
ⲡⲙⲁ ⲉⲧⲙ̄ⲙⲁⲩ	*there*
ⲙⲏⲧⲉ	(f. noun, *middle*)
ⲉ ⲧⲙⲏⲧⲉ	*to, into the midst*
ⲛ̄ ⲧⲙⲏⲧⲉ	*in the midst, between*
ⲉⲃⲟⲗ ⲛ̄ ⲧⲙⲏⲧⲉ	*from the midst*
ϩⲛ̄ ⲧⲙⲏⲧⲉ	*in the midst, between*
ⲉⲃⲟⲗ ϩⲛ̄ ⲧⲙⲏⲧⲉ	*from the midst*
ϩⲓ ⲧⲙⲏⲧⲉ	*in, through the midst*
ⲙⲁⲩ	(noun, *the place there*)
ⲙ̄ⲙⲁⲩ	*there*
ⲉⲃⲟⲗ ⲙ̄ⲙⲁⲩ	*from there (whence)*
ⲉⲙⲁⲩ	*to there (thither)*
ⲡⲉ	(f. noun, *heaven*)
ⲉⲧⲡⲉ	*upward*
ⲛ̄ ⲧⲡⲉ	*above*
ϩⲛ̄ ⲧⲡⲉ	*above*
(ⲛ̄) ⲥⲁ—ⲧⲡⲉ	*above*
ϩⲓ ⲧⲡⲉ	*above*
ϫⲓⲛ ⲧⲡⲉ	*from above*
ⲡⲁϩⲟⲩ	(m. noun, *back*)
ⲉⲡⲁϩⲟⲩ	*back, rearward*
ϣⲁ—ⲡⲁϩⲟⲩ	*behind, after*
ⲛ̄ ⲥⲁ—ⲡⲁϩⲟⲩ	*behind, from behind*
ϩⲓ ⲡⲁϩⲟⲩ	*behind*
ⲥⲁ	(m. noun, *side, part*)
ⲡⲉⲓⲥⲁ ⲡⲁⲓ	*this way and that*
ⲡⲓⲥⲁ ⲡⲓⲕⲉⲥⲁ	*this way and that*

ⲥⲁ *(continued)*	
ⲕⲉⲥⲁ	*apart, elsewhere*
ⲛ̄ ⲥⲁ ⲥⲁ ⲛⲓⲙ	*every which way*
ⲛ̄ ⲥⲁ ⲟⲩⲥⲁ	*apart, alone*
ⲛ̄ ⲥⲁ ⲗⲁⲁⲩ ⲛ̄ ⲥⲁ	*on any (no) side*
ϣⲱⲓ	(m. noun, *what is high*)
ⲉ ⲡϣⲱⲓ	*upward*
ⲉⲃⲟⲗ ⲙ̄ ⲡϣⲱⲓ	*from above*
ⲥⲁ—ⲡϣⲱⲓ	*upward*
ⲉⲃⲟⲗ ⲥⲁ—ⲡϣⲱⲓ	*from above*
ϩⲏ	(f. noun, *front*)
ⲉ ⲑⲏ	*ahead, forward*
ϩⲁ ⲑⲏ	*in front of, before*
ϩⲓ ⲑⲏ	*to, at front, forward*
ϩⲓ ϩⲏ	*to, at front, forward*
ϩⲟ	(m. noun, *face*)
ϩⲟ ⲙⲛ̄ ϩⲟ	*face to face*
ϩⲟ ⲟⲩⲃⲉ ϩⲟ	*face to face*
ϩⲟ ϩⲓ ϩⲟ	*face to face*
ⲛ̄ ϩⲟ	*by face, by sight*
ⲙ̄ ⲡϩⲟ	*by face, by sight*
ϩⲙ̄ ⲡϩⲟ	*by face, by sight*
ϩⲁ ⲛ̄ ϩⲟ	*away from*
ϩⲟⲩⲛ	(m. noun, *inside*)
ⲉϩⲟⲩⲛ	*into*
ⲛ̄ϩⲟⲩⲛ	*within*
ⲥⲁ—ϩⲟⲩⲛ	*within*
ϣⲁ ϩⲟⲩⲛ	*inward*
ϩⲓ ϩⲟⲩⲛ	*within*
ϩⲣⲁⲓ	(m. noun, *upper part*)
ⲉϩⲣⲁⲓ	*up*
ⲛ̄ϩⲣⲁⲓ	*above*
ⲥⲁ-ϩⲣⲁⲓ	*above*
ϣⲁ ϩⲣⲁⲓ	*upward*
ϩⲓ ϩⲣⲁⲓ	*upward*

ϩⲣⲁⲓ	(m. noun, *lower part*)
ⲉϩⲣⲁⲓ	*down*
ⲛ̅ϩⲣⲁⲓ	*below*
ⲥⲁ-ϩⲣⲁⲓ	*below*

Temporal Adverbs

Introductory Note: Many of these adverbial expressions consist of a noun of time preceded by a preposition. The basic form may be a noun, adjective, or adverb, e.g., ⲉⲛⲉϩ is all three.

ⲃⲣ̅ⲣⲉ	(adj. or noun, *new, young*)
ⲛ̅ ⲃⲣ̅ⲣⲉ	*recently*
ⲉⲛⲉϩ	*forever*
ϣⲁ—ⲉⲛⲉϩ	*forever*
ϣⲁ—ⲛⲓⲉⲛⲉϩ	*forever*
ϣⲁ ⲉⲛⲉϩ ⲛ̅ ⲟⲩⲟⲉⲓϣ	*forever*
ϫⲓⲛ ⲉⲛⲉϩ	*from of old*
ⲕⲟⲩⲓ	(noun or adj., *small, young*)
ⲛ̅ ⲕⲉⲕⲟⲩⲓ	*yet a little*
ⲙⲛ̅ⲛ̅ⲥⲁ ⲟⲩⲕⲟⲩⲓ	*after a little while*
ϩⲁⲑⲏ ⲛ̅ ⲟⲩⲕⲟⲩⲓ	*a little while before*
ⲡⲣⲟⲥ ⲟⲩⲕⲟⲩⲓ	*for a little, occasionally*
ⲙ̅ⲙⲏⲛⲉ	*daily*
ⲟⲛ	*again*
ⲡⲁϩⲟⲩ	(m. noun, *back*)
ϩⲁ ⲡⲁϩⲟⲩ	*formerly*
ⲣⲟⲙⲡⲉ	(f. noun, *year*)
ⲉⲓⲥ ϩⲉⲛⲣⲟⲙⲡⲉ	*years ago*
ⲛ̅ ⲟⲩⲣⲟⲙⲡⲉ	*for a year*
(ⲛ̅) ⲧⲣⲟⲙⲡⲉ	*this year*
ⲧⲛ̅ⲣⲟⲙⲡⲉ, ⲧⲣ̅ⲣⲟⲙⲡⲉ, ⲧⲉⲣⲟⲙⲡⲉ	*each year, annually*

ⲣⲁⲥⲧⲉ	(m. noun, *morrow*)
ⲡⲣⲁⲥⲧⲉ	*tomorrow*
ⲉ ⲣⲁⲥⲧⲉ	*tomorrow*
ⲛ̣̄ⲉ ⲣⲁⲥⲧⲉ	*tomorrow*
ⲙ̄ ⲡⲉϥⲣⲁⲥⲧⲉ	*tomorrow*
ⲛ̄ⲥⲁ ⲣⲁⲥⲧⲉ	*after tomorrow*
ϣⲁ (ⲡⲉϥ)ⲣⲁⲥⲧⲉ	*until tomorrow*
ϩⲛ̄ ⲣⲁⲥⲧⲉ	*tomorrow*
ⲣⲟⲩϩⲉ	(m. noun, *evening*)
ⲉ/ⲛ̄/ϩⲓ ⲣⲟⲩϩⲉ	*in the evening*
ϣⲁ ⲣⲟⲩϩⲉ	*until the evening*
ⲥⲁ	(m. noun, *side, part*)
ⲙⲛ̄ⲛ̄ⲥⲱⲥ	*afterward*
ⲧⲉ, ⲧⲏ	(m. noun, *time, season*)
ⲙ̄ ⲡⲉϥⲧⲉ	*at the right time*
ϩⲙ̄ ⲡⲉϥⲧⲉ	*at the right time*
ⲉ ⲡⲧⲉ	*in time*
ⲟⲩⲛⲟⲩ	(f. noun, *hour*)
ⲛ̄ ⲧⲉⲛⲟⲩ	*immediately*
ϩⲛ̄ ⲧⲉⲩⲛⲟⲩ	*immediately*
ⲡⲣⲟⲥ ⲧⲉⲩⲛⲟⲩ	*for an hour*
ⲧⲉⲛⲟⲩ	*immediately, now*
ⲉ ⲧⲉⲩⲛⲟⲩ	*immediately*
ϣⲁ ⲧⲉⲛⲟⲩ	*until now*
ϫⲓⲛ ⲧⲉⲛⲟⲩ	*from now*
ⲟⲩⲟⲉⲓϣ	(m. noun, *time, occasion*)
ⲡⲉⲟⲩⲟⲉⲓϣ ⲉⲧⲙ̄ⲙⲁⲩ	*at that time*
ⲉ ⲟⲩⲟⲉⲓϣ	*at a time*
ⲉⲓⲥ ⲟⲩⲟⲉⲓϣ	*since*
ⲙⲛ̄ⲛ̄ⲥⲁ ⲟⲩⲟⲉⲓϣ	*after*
ⲛ̄ ⲟⲩⲟⲉⲓϣ ⲛⲓⲙ	*always*
ⲙ̄ ⲡⲓⲟⲩⲟⲉⲓϣ/ⲙ̄ ⲡⲉⲟⲩⲟⲉⲓϣ	*at this time, formerly*
ⲛ̄ ⲟⲩⲟⲩⲟⲉⲓϣ	*on a time (past)*
ϣⲁ ⲟⲩⲟⲉⲓϣ	*until, during, later on*
ϩⲁⲑⲏ ⲟⲩⲟⲉⲓϣ	*before*

ⲟⲩⲟⲉⲓϣ *(continued)*	
ϩⲙ̄ ⲡⲉⲟⲩⲟⲉⲓϣ	*in, during*
ϫⲓⲛ ⲟⲩⲟⲉⲓϣ	*since, from*
ⲕⲁⲧⲁ ⲟⲩⲟⲉⲓϣ	*from time to time*
ⲡⲁⲣⲁ ⲡⲉⲟⲩⲟⲉⲓϣ	*beyond*
ⲡⲣⲟⲥ ⲟⲩⲟⲉⲓϣ	*for, during*
ⲟⲩϣⲏ	(f. noun, *night*)
ⲛ̄ ⲟⲩⲟⲩϣⲏ	*during a night*
ⲛ̄ ⲧⲉⲩϣⲏ	*by night*
ⲟⲩⲱϩⲙ̄	(verb, *repeat, answer*)
ⲡⲟⲩⲱϩⲙ̄	*again*
ϩⲧⲟⲟⲩⲉ	(m. noun, *dawn*)
ⲉ/ⲛ̄/ϩⲓ/ⲉ ϩⲛ̄ ϩⲧⲟⲟⲩⲉ	*at dawn*
ϣⲁ ϩⲧⲟⲟⲩⲉ	*until dawn*
ϫⲓⲛ ϩⲧⲟⲟⲩⲉ	*from dawn*
ϩⲟⲟⲩ	(m. noun, *day*)
ϩⲟⲟⲩ	*today*
ⲙ̄ ⲡⲉϩⲟⲟⲩ	*by day*
ⲛ̄ ⲟⲩϩⲟⲟⲩ	*for a day*
ϩⲛ̄ ⲟⲩϩⲟⲟⲩ ⲉⲃⲟⲗ ϩⲛ̄ ⲟⲩϩⲟⲟⲩ	*from day to day*
ϣⲁ ⲡⲉϩⲟⲟⲩ	*until the day*
ϩⲙ̄ ⲡⲉϩⲟⲟⲩ	*in day*
ϫⲓⲛ ϩⲟⲟⲩ ⲉ ϩⲟⲟⲩ	*from day to day*
ⲟⲩϩⲟⲟⲩ ⲉⲃⲟⲗ ϩⲛ̄ ⲟⲩϩⲟⲟⲩ	*on a certain day*
ϩⲟⲟⲩ ϩⲟⲟⲩ	*from day to day*
ϣⲱⲣⲡ̄	(verb, *be early*)
ⲛ̄ ϣⲱⲣⲡ̄ (ⲛ̄ ϣⲟⲣⲡ̄)	*early*
ⲛ̄ ϣⲟⲣⲡ̄	*at first; formerly*
ⲕⲁⲧⲁ ϣⲟⲣⲡ̄	*as formerly*
ϫⲓⲛ (ⲛ̄) ϣⲟⲣⲡ̄	*from the beginning*
ϫⲓⲛ ⲉ ϣⲟⲣⲡ̄	*from the beginning*
ϩⲁⲉ	(noun, adj., *last thing, end*)
ⲉ ⲡϩⲁⲉ	*at last, finally*
ⲙ̄ ⲡϩⲁⲉ	*at last, finally*

ϩⲁⲉ *(continued)*

ⲛ̄ ⲑⲁⲉ	*at last, finally*
ⲛ̄ ϩⲁⲉ	*at last, finally*
ⲉϫⲛ̄ ϩⲁⲉ	*at last, finally*
ϩⲛ̄ ⲑⲁⲉ	*at last, finally*
ϣⲁ ϩⲁⲉ	*until the last, at the last*
ϣⲁ ⲑⲁⲉ	*until the last, at the last*

ϩⲏ	(f. noun, *front part, beginning*)
ⲛ̄ⲥⲁ ⲑⲏ	*formerly, henceforth*
ϫⲓⲛ ⲛ̄ ϩⲏ	*from the beginning*

Other Adverbs

ⲉⲧⲃⲉ	(prep. *because of*)
ⲉⲧⲃⲉ ⲡⲁⲓ	*therefore*

PART FOUR

THE VERBAL SYSTEM

CLASSES OF INFINITIVES

Introductory Notes

1. Coptic infinitives are built from consonantal roots, in a way that is similar to the "radicals" of Hebrew and Aramaic. In all three languages, it is possible to speak of the consonantal skeleton of the infinitive or verb. Unlike Hebrew and Aramaic, Coptic vowels are written as letters in concert with the consonants.
2. Infinitives can be grouped into seven major morphological classes depending on the number of consonants and shifts in the vowels.[1] There are a number of minor classes and some infinitives that do not easily fall into classes. Some of the minor classes or subclasses are included below; however, beginning students should first concentrate on the basic patterns that are listed. The following arrangement of classes represents an attempt to provide an order that will assist students as they learn the language.

   NOTE: c = consonant (radical)

   a. The backbone of the infinitive is the presence of one to five consonants. They remain constant and are the basis for entries in most dictionaries (much like Hebrew lexica).
   b. There is a distinctive vowel in these classes. The first three classes use ⲱ, the next three ⲟ, and the final class ⲓ. Vowels shift within the infinitive. The classes are based on the common shifts of the vowels as the infinitive moves from one state to another. I have clustered the subclasses or minor classes that use the same vowel shifts beneath the major entry.
3. Coptic infinitives have four states[2]:

   Absolute (the basic form of the infinitive)
   Prenominal (the form of the infinitive when it is bound to a following noun)
   Prepronominal (the form of the infinitive before a pronominal suffix)
   Qualitative or stative (this describes a state or condition)

   NOTES:

   1.) Students of Greek may think of the four states along lines that are similar to but not identical to the principal parts of the Greek verb. The similarity lies in the fact that students must learn multiple forms for each infinitive or verb. The dissimilarity consists of function: the Coptic states may reflect the different forms of an infinitive without suggesting a shift in tense while the principal parts of a Greek verb represent different tenses and voices.
   2.) Not all infinitives have all four states.
   3.) Infinitives may have more than one form for a specific state. Only the basic patterns are listed below. Students will need to consult a lexicon for full lists.

[1] I am following the analysis of B. Layton, *A Coptic Grammar* (2nd ed., Porta Linguarum Orinetalium 20; Wiesbaden: Harrosowitz, 2004) 151-57 or §§186-93, for the seven classes.

[2] State is the standard name for the four forms. They are also known as stem patterns.

5.) The states are directly associated with the different verbal systems in Coptic. The tripartite system uses the absolute, pronominal, and prepronominal states. The bipartite system uses the absolute and qualitative states, but not the pronominal or prepronominal states except for ⲟⲩⲱϣ (*wish, love*). While the first future is related to the first present, it takes the pronominal and prepronominal forms of the infinitive.
5.) Some infinitives also have a construct participle that is known as the *participium conjunctivum*, abbreviated p.c.

4. Coptic uses a significant number of Greek verbs. Greco-Coptic infinitives appear in a fixed form that approximates the second person, singular form of the imperative in Greek, e.g., ⲃⲁⲡⲧⲓⲍⲉ (βάπτιζε [*baptize*]), ⲉⲩⲁⲅⲅⲉⲗⲓⲍⲉ (εὐαγγέλιζε [*announce the good news, evangelize*]), ⲡⲓⲥⲧⲉⲩⲉ (πίστευε [*believe*]).

Infinitives with ⲱ

	Absolute	Prenominal	Prepronominal	Qualitative
1.	ⲥⲱⲥ^{e}ⲥ (Three consonants with ⲱ)			
	ⲥⲱⲧⲙ̄	ⲥⲉⲧⲙ̄—	ⲥⲟⲧⲙ=	
	ⲥⲱⲧⲡ̄	ⲥⲉⲧⲡ̄—	ⲥⲟⲧⲡ=	ⲥⲟⲧⲡ̄
	Initial ⲙ or ⲛ (ⲱ shifts to ⲟⲩ)			
	ⲙⲟⲩⲟⲩⲧ	ⲙⲉⲩⲧ—	ⲙⲟⲟⲩⲧ=	
	ⲛⲟⲩϩⲙ̄	ⲛⲉϩⲙ̄—	ⲛⲁϩⲙ=	ⲛⲁϩⲙ̄
	Second Radical is ϩ or ϣ			
	ⲛⲟⲩϩⲙ̄	ⲛⲉϩⲙ̄—	ⲛⲁϩⲙ=	ⲛⲁϩⲙ̄
	ⲡⲱϩⲧ̄	ⲡⲉϩⲧ—	ⲡⲁϩⲧ=	ⲡⲁϩⲧ
	ⲥⲱϣⲧ	ⲥⲉϣⲧ—	ⲥⲟϣⲧ=	ⲥⲁϣⲧ
	ⲧⲱϩⲙ̄	ⲧⲉϩⲙ̄—	ⲧⲁϩⲙ=	ⲧⲁϩⲙ̄
	ⲟⲩⲱϣⲥ	ⲟⲩⲉϣⲥ—	ⲟⲩⲟϣⲥ=	ⲟⲩⲟϣⲥ
	ⲟⲩⲱϩⲙ̄	ⲟⲩⲉϩⲙ̄—	ⲟⲩⲁϩⲙ=	ⲟⲩⲟϩⲙ̄

NOTES:

1. This is the most common class of infinitive.
2. They may be either transitive or intransitive.

	Absolute	Prenominal	Prepronominal	Qualitative
2.	ⲥⲱⲥ (Two consonants with ⲱ)			
	ⲃⲱⲕ			ⲃⲏⲕ
	ⲕⲱⲧ	ⲕⲉⲧ—	ⲕⲟⲧ=	ⲕⲏⲧ
	ⲡⲱⲧ			ⲡⲏⲧ
	ⲟⲩⲱⲛ	ⲟⲩⲛ̄—		ⲟⲩⲏⲛ
	ϣⲱⲡ	ϣⲉⲡ—	ϣⲟⲡ=	ϣⲏⲡ
	ϩⲱⲛ			ϩⲏⲛ

Absolute	Prenominal	Prepronominal	Qualitative
ϩⲱⲡ	ϩⲉⲡ—	ϩⲟⲡ⸗	ϩⲏⲡ
ϫⲱⲕ	ϫⲉⲕ—	ϫⲟⲕ⸗	ϫⲏⲕ

ⲙ or ⲛ + ⲟⲩ + Consonant (ⲱ shifts to ⲟⲩ)

ⲙⲟⲩⲣ	ⲙⲉⲣ—	ⲙⲟⲣ⸗	ⲙⲏⲣ
ⲙⲟⲩϩ	ⲙⲉϩ—	ⲙⲁϩ⸗	ⲙⲉϩ

Consonant + ⲱ+ Final ϩ or ϣ (Vowel frequently shifts to ⲁ before the prepronominal form)

ⲙⲟⲩϩ	ⲙⲉϩ—	ⲙⲁϩ⸗	ⲙⲉϩ
ⲡⲱϣ	ⲡⲉϣ—	ⲡⲁϣ⸗	ⲡⲏϣ
ⲟⲩⲱϣ	ⲟⲩⲉϣ—	ⲟⲩⲁϣ⸗	
ⲟⲩⲱϩ	ⲟⲩⲉϩ—	ⲟⲩⲁϩ⸗	ⲟⲩⲏϩ

NOTES:

1. These infinitives may be either transitive or intransitive.
2. They express an action.

ⲥⲱⲥⲉ (Consonant, stressed ⲱ, consonant, unstressed ⲉ)

ⲕⲱⲧⲉ	ⲕⲉⲧ—	ⲕⲟⲧ⸗	ⲕⲏⲧ

NOTE: Some relate this to the first class; however, there are only two consonants.

ⲱⲥ (Vowel plus consonant)

ⲱⲡ	ⲉⲡ—	ⲟⲡ⸗	ⲏⲡ
ⲱϣ	ⲉϣ—	ⲟϣ⸗	

NOTE: This could be a separate class since it only has one consonant; however, the vowel shifts are the same as those in the second class.

3. ⲥⲱⲱⲥⲉ (Three consonants with ⲱ: consonant, glottal stop as second consonant [marked by two vowels], consonant)

ⲡⲱⲱⲛⲉ	ⲡⲉⲉⲛⲉ—	ⲡⲟⲟⲛⲉ⸗	ⲡⲟⲟⲛⲉ
ϣⲱⲱϭⲉ	ϣⲉⲉϭⲉ—	ϣⲟⲟϭ⸗	ϣⲟⲟϭⲉ

Infinitives with ⲟ

4. ⲥⲟⲥⲥᵉⲥ (Reduplication of consonants with ⲟ)

ⲥⲟⲗⲥⲗ̄	ⲥⲗ̄ⲥⲗ̄—	ⲥⲗ̄ⲥⲱⲗ⸗	ⲥⲗ̄ⲥⲱⲗ
ϣⲧⲟⲣⲧⲣ̄	ϣⲧⲣ̄ⲧⲣ̄—	ϣⲧⲣ̄ⲧⲱⲣ⸗	ϣⲧⲣ̄ⲧⲱⲣ

	Absolute	Prenominal	Prepronominal	Qualitative
5.	Initial ⲧ and final ⲟ			
	ⲧⲃ̅ⲃⲟ	ⲧⲃ̅ⲃⲉ—	ⲧⲃ̅ⲃⲟ⸗	ⲧⲃ̅ⲃⲏⲩ
	ⲧⲁⲕⲟ	ⲧⲁⲕⲉ—	ⲧⲁⲕⲟ⸗	ⲧⲁⲕⲏⲩ
	ⲧⲁⲗⲟ	ⲧⲁⲗⲉ—	ⲧⲁⲗⲟ⸗	ⲧⲁⲗⲏⲩ
	ⲧⲁⲙⲟ	ⲧⲁⲙⲉ—	ⲧⲁⲙⲟ⸗	
	ⲧⲛ̅ⲛⲟⲟⲩ	ⲧⲛ̅ⲛⲉⲩ—	ⲧⲛ̅ⲛⲟⲟⲩ⸗	
	ⲧⲥⲁⲃⲟ	ⲧⲥⲁⲃⲉ—	ⲧⲥⲁⲃⲟ⸗	ⲧⲥⲁⲃⲏⲩ
	ⲧⲁϫⲣⲟ	ⲧⲁϫⲣⲉ—	ⲧⲁϫⲣⲟ⸗	ⲧⲁϫⲣⲏⲩ
	Initial ⲧ followed by ϣ results in ϫ			
	ϫⲟ	ϫⲉ—	ϫⲟ⸗	ϫⲏⲩ
	ϫⲡⲓⲟ	ϫⲡⲓⲉ—	ϫⲡⲓⲟ⸗	ϫⲡⲓⲏⲧ
	ϫⲡⲟ	ϫⲡⲉ—	ϫⲡⲟ⸗	
	Lost Initial ⲧ			
	ⲕⲧⲟ	ⲕⲧⲉ—	ⲕⲧⲟ⸗	ⲕⲧⲏⲩ

NOTES:

1. Most of these verbs are transitive.
2. They are causatives that originally came from a compound causative that used a form of ϯ and a verbal form that was inflected by means of a suffix.

6. ^{e}ⲥⲥⲟⲥ (Three consonants with ⲟ)

Absolute	Prenominal	Prepronominal	Qualitative
ⲙ̅ⲕⲁϩ			ⲙⲟⲕϩ̅
ⲙ̅ⲧⲟⲛ			ⲙⲟⲧⲛ̅
ⲛ̅ϣⲟⲧ			ⲛ̅ⲁϣⲧ
ⲟⲩⲟⲡ			ⲟⲩⲁⲁⲃ

NOTES:

1. Intransitive verbs
2. Verbs in this class express entrance into or being in a state.

Infinitives with ⲓ

7. ⲥⲓⲥⲉ (Three consonants with ⲓ; the final consonant is a weak ⲧ that appears as ⲉ in the absolute and qualitative states)

Absolute	Prenominal	Prepronominal	Qualitative
ⲉⲓϣⲉ	ⲉϣⲧ—	ⲁϣⲧ⸗	ⲁϣⲉ
ⲙⲓⲥⲉ	ⲙⲉⲥ(ⲧ)—	ⲙⲁⲥⲧ⸗	ⲙⲟⲥⲉ
ⲡⲓⲥⲉ	ⲡⲉⲥⲧ—	ⲡⲁⲥⲧ⸗	ⲡⲟⲥⲉ
ϫⲓⲥⲉ	ϫⲉⲥⲧ—	ϫⲁⲥⲧ⸗	ϫⲟⲥⲉ

Absolute	Prenominal	Prepronominal	Qualitative
Irregular			
ⲉⲓⲙⲉ			
ⲉⲓⲛⲉ	ⲛ̄—	ⲛ̄ⲧ=	
ⲉⲓⲣⲉ	ⲣ̄—	ⲁⲁ=	ⲟ
ϣⲓⲛⲉ	ϣⲛ̄—	ϣⲛ̄ⲧ=	
ϭⲓⲛⲉ	ϭⲛ̄—	ϭⲛ̄ⲧ=	

NOTES:
1. Transitive and intransitive
2. Express an action

ⲥⲓⲥ (Two consonant variation; the final consonant is a weak ⲧ that is only evident in the prepronominal state)

ϣⲓ	ϣⲓ—	ϣⲓⲧ=	ϣⲏⲩ
ϥⲓ	ϥⲓ—	ϥⲓⲧ=	ϥⲏⲩ
ϫⲓ	ϫⲓ—	ϫⲓⲧ=	ϫⲏⲩ
Irregular			
ϯ	ϯ—	ⲧⲁⲁ=	ⲧⲟ

NOTES:
1. Transitive and intransitive
2. Qualitative form: ⲥⲏⲩ

Infinitives with ⲉ and ⲩ

Rare

Monosyllabic Infinitives

ⲥⲱ (Consonant plus vowel)

ⲉⲓⲱ	ⲉⲓⲁ—	ⲉⲓⲁⲁ=	ⲉⲓⲏ
ⲕⲱ	ⲕⲁ—	ⲕⲁⲁ=	ⲕⲏ
ⲥⲱ	ⲥⲉ—	ⲥⲟⲟ=	
ϫⲱ	ϫⲉ—	ϫⲟⲟ=	

NOTE: These do not constitute a formal class, but are listed together for convenience. While the pattern of consonant plus vowel is infrequent, the infinitives above are common.

VERBAL PATTERNS AND CONJUGATIONS

INTRODUCTORY NOTES

1. There are two basic verbal patterns in Coptic: the tripartite (non-durative) and the bipartite (durative).
   a. The non-durative or tripartite pattern does not qualify the action with a notion of durativity: it simply posits the action. The durative or bipartite pattern conveys continuous action, a state of existence, or imminent action.
   b. The tripartite pattern has three components, while the bipartite pattern consists of two components.
   c. The two names thus accentuate either the *Aktionsart* of the tenses (non-durative versus durative) or the constitutions of the tenses (bipartite versus tripartite).
2. The tripartite or non-durative pattern consists of three elements: a conjugation base, the subject, and the infinitive which may occur in the absolute, the prenominal, or the prepronominal states, as noted above.
   a. The conjugations in the tripartite system belong to one of two sub-patterns: five main clause or sentence conjugations and five subordinate clause conjugations.
   b. The main clause or sentence conjugations are conjugations that form complete sentences. Each conjugation has a separate positive and a negative conjugation except the "not yet" conjugation which has only the negative. It is possible to convert each of these conjugations with four converters (see below) except for the injunctive that has no conversions.
   c. The subordinate clause conjugations form dependent clauses and must therefore be used in conjunction with another conjugation. Unlike the main clause or sentence conjugations, they do not have separate positive and negative conjugations; rather, they use a common morpheme (—ⲧⲙ̄—) to negate the infinitive except for the future conjunctive of result which does not appear in a negative form (there is one contested example). The subordinate clauses fall into two groups: adverbial clauses (the temporal, conditional, and "until") and conjunctive clauses (conjunctive and future conjunctive of result). Subordinate clause conjugations do not take converters.
3. The bipartite pattern consists of the subject and the infinitive which may appear in either the absolute or qualitative form but not in the prenominal or prepronominal form, as noted above.
   a. The bipartite pattern contains the first present tense and the imperfect tense (that is built from the first present). Both tenses take Coptic converters.
   b. The first future is also built from the first present, although it does not follow the bipartite pattern in a number of ways: it uses the future auxiliary —ⲛⲁ— giving it three components, it is not durative, and it takes the pronominal and prepronimal forms of the infinitives. Since the morphology is directly related to the first present, we will treat it as part of the bipartite pattern.
   c. The First Present, Imperfect, and First Future are all negated by either ⲛ̄ ... ⲁⲛ or ⲁⲛ.

4. In addition to these two basic verbal patterns, there are several anomalous verbal patterns which I have placed last.
   a. The Imperative. The simple imperative is not part of either system although it is more like the tripartite system since it is not limited by the restrictions of the bipartite system.
   b. The Inflected (Causative) Infinitive. Properly speaking, this is not a conjugation but the infinitive ⲧⲣⲉ—. It is sometimes causative (*cause to ...*) and sometimes it is not. The infinitive may stand in either the pronominal or prepronominal state. The infinitive ⲧⲣⲉ— may be used in combination with both the conjugations of the tripartite pattern and the conjugations of the bipartite pattern.
5. Specific Morphological Comments.
   a. The singular forms of the verbs make a distinction in gender in the second and third persons. The plural forms of the verbs do not make any distinctions in gender.
   b. The second feminine singular personal prefix is ⲧⲉ—, but there is a variant prefix ⲧⲣ̄—. The result is that there are multiple forms of the second feminine singular in the First Perfect, Negative First Perfect, First Present, and First Future.

Tripartite or Non-Durative Pattern

Sentence or Main Clause Conjugations

Positive	Negative
First Perfect	Negative First Perfect
————	"Not yet"
Habitual (*Praesens Consuetudinis*)[3]	Negative Habitual
Third Future[4]	Negative Third Future
Injunctive (Optative)[5]	Negative Injunctive

Subordinate Clause Conjugations

Temporal[6]
Conditional
"Until"[7]
Conjunctive
Future Conjunctive of Result (*Finalis*)

NOTE: There are no special negative bases. All use —ⲧⲙ̄— to negate the verb (except the Future Conjuctive of Result that lacks a negative).

[3] Some call this the aorist. The name may be misleading for those who know Greek grammar.
[4] Some call this the optative.
[5] Some call this the jussive.
[6] Some call this the precursive.
[7] Some call this the limitative.

Bipartite or Durative Pattern

First Present
Imperfect[8]
First Future[9]

Anomalous Patterns

Imperative
Inflected Infinitive

Summary of the Tripartite and Bipartite Patterns

	Tripartite	**Bipartite**
Components	Conjugation base Subject Infinitive	 Subject Infinitive
Aspect	Non-durative	Durative
States of the Infinitive	Absolute Prenominal Prepronominal	Absolute Qualitative
Adverbial Predicate		Adverb Prepositional Phrase
Negation Sentence Conjugations Clause Conjugations	 Negative Conjugations —ⲧⲙ̄—	(ⲛ̄) ... ⲁⲛ
Indefinite Subject	No special requirement	ⲟⲩⲛ̄— or ⲙⲛ̄— Required for Present Tense, but not Imperfect
Converters Sentence Conjugations Clause Conjugations	 Full conversions No conversions	Full conversions

[8] This is based on the first present. It is a preterite conversion of the first present.
[9] This is an anomalous tense in the bipartite pattern (see above). The second future and *imperfectum futuri* are based on it.

Tripartite or Non-Durative Pattern

Sentence or Main Clause Conjugations

	First Perfect	*Negative First Perfect*
	Singular	
1	ⲁⲓⲥⲱⲧⲙ̄	ⲙ̄ⲡⲓⲥⲱⲧⲙ̄
2m	ⲁⲕⲥⲱⲧⲙ̄	ⲙ̄ⲡⲉⲕⲥⲱⲧⲙ̄
2f	ⲁⲣⲥⲱⲧⲙ̄[10]	ⲙ̄ⲡⲉⲥⲱⲧⲙ̄[11]
3m	ⲁϥⲥⲱⲧⲙ̄	ⲙ̄ⲡⲉϥⲥⲱⲧⲙ̄
3f	ⲁⲥⲥⲱⲧⲙ̄	ⲙ̄ⲡⲉⲥⲥⲱⲧⲙ̄

	First Perfect	*Negative First Perfect*
	Plural	
1	ⲁⲛⲥⲱⲧⲙ̄	ⲙ̄ⲡⲉⲛⲥⲱⲧⲙ̄
2	ⲁⲧⲉⲧⲛ̄ⲥⲱⲧⲙ̄	ⲙ̄ⲡⲉⲧⲛ̄ⲥⲱⲧⲙ̄
3	ⲁⲩⲥⲱⲧⲙ̄	ⲙ̄ⲡⲟⲩⲥⲱⲧⲙ̄
	ⲁ—ⲡⲣⲱⲙⲉ ⲥⲱⲧⲙ̄	ⲙ̄ⲡⲉ—ⲡⲣⲱⲙⲉ ⲥⲱⲧⲙ̄

		"Not yet"
	Singular	
1	______________	ⲙ̄ⲡⲁϯⲥⲱⲧⲙ̄
2m	______________	ⲙ̄ⲡⲁⲧⲕ̄ⲥⲱⲧⲙ̄
2f	______________	ⲙ̄ⲡⲁⲧⲉⲥⲱⲧⲙ̄
3m	______________	ⲙ̄ⲡⲁⲧϥ̄ⲥⲱⲧⲙ̄
3f	______________	ⲙ̄ⲡⲁⲧⲥ̄ⲥⲱⲧⲙ̄
	Plural	
1	______________	ⲙ̄ⲡⲁⲧⲛ̄ⲥⲱⲧⲙ̄
2	______________	ⲙ̄ⲡⲁⲧⲉⲧⲛ̄ⲥⲱⲧⲙ̄
3	______________	ⲙ̄ⲡⲁⲧⲟⲩⲥⲱⲧⲙ̄
		ⲙ̄ⲡⲁⲧⲉ—ⲡⲣⲱⲙⲉ ⲥⲱⲧⲙ̄

[10] Variants ⲁⲥⲱⲧⲙ̄ or ⲁⲣⲉⲥⲱⲧⲙ̄.
[11] Variant ⲙ̄ⲡⲣ̄ⲥⲱⲧⲙ̄.

	Habitual	*Negative Habitual*
	Singular	
1	ϣⲁⲓⲥⲱⲧⲙ̄	ⲙⲉⲓⲥⲱⲧⲙ̄
2m	ϣⲁⲕⲥⲱⲧⲙ̄	ⲙⲉⲕⲥⲱⲧⲙ̄
2f	ϣⲁⲣ(ⲉ)ⲥⲱⲧⲙ̄	ⲙⲉⲣⲉⲥⲱⲧⲙ̄
3m	ϣⲁϥⲥⲱⲧⲙ̄	ⲙⲉϥⲥⲱⲧⲙ̄
3f	ϣⲁⲥⲥⲱⲧⲙ̄	ⲙⲉⲥⲥⲱⲧⲙ̄
	Plural	
1	ϣⲁⲛⲥⲱⲧⲙ̄	ⲙⲉⲛⲥⲱⲧⲙ̄
2	ϣⲁⲧⲉⲧⲛ̄ⲥⲱⲧⲙ̄	ⲙⲉⲧⲉⲧⲛ̄ⲥⲱⲧⲙ̄
3	ϣⲁⲩⲥⲱⲧⲙ̄	ⲙⲉⲩⲥⲱⲧⲙ̄
	ϣⲁⲣⲉ—ⲡⲣⲱⲙⲉ ⲥⲱⲧⲙ̄	ⲙⲉⲣⲉ—ⲡⲣⲱⲙⲉ ⲥⲱⲧⲙ̄

	Third Future	*Negative Third Future*
	Singular	
1	ⲉⲓⲉⲥⲱⲧⲙ̄	ⲛ̄ⲛⲁⲥⲱⲧⲙ̄
2m	ⲉⲕⲉⲥⲱⲧⲙ̄	ⲛ̄ⲛⲉⲕⲥⲱⲧⲙ̄
2f	ⲉⲣⲉⲥⲱⲧⲙ̄	ⲛ̄ⲛⲉⲥⲱⲧⲙ̄
3m	ⲉϥⲉⲥⲱⲧⲙ̄	ⲛ̄ⲛⲉϥⲥⲱⲧⲙ̄
3f	ⲉⲥⲉⲥⲱⲧⲙ̄	ⲛ̄ⲛⲉⲥⲥⲱⲧⲙ̄
	Plural	
1	ⲉⲛⲉⲥⲱⲧⲙ̄	ⲛ̄ⲛⲉⲛⲥⲱⲧⲙ̄
2	ⲉⲧⲉⲧⲛⲉⲥⲱⲧⲙ̄	ⲛ̄ⲛⲉⲧⲛ̄ⲥⲱⲧⲙ̄
3	ⲉⲩⲉⲥⲱⲧⲙ̄	ⲛ̄ⲛⲉⲩⲥⲱⲧⲙ̄
	ⲉⲣⲉ—ⲡⲣⲱⲙⲉ ⲥⲱⲧⲙ̄	ⲛ̄ⲛⲉ-ⲡⲣⲱⲙⲉ ⲥⲱⲧⲙ̄

	Injunctive	*Negative Injunctive*[12]
	Singular	
1	ⲙⲁⲣⲓⲥⲱⲧⲙ̄	ⲙ̄ⲡⲣ̄ⲧⲣⲁⲥⲱⲧⲙ̄
2m	______	______
2f	______	______
3m	ⲙⲁⲣⲉϥⲥⲱⲧⲙ̄	ⲙ̄ⲡⲣ̄ⲧⲣⲉϥⲥⲱⲧⲙ̄
3f	ⲙⲁⲣⲉⲥⲥⲱⲧⲙ̄	ⲙ̄ⲡⲣ̄ⲧⲣⲉⲥⲥⲱⲧⲙ̄
	Plural	
1	ⲙⲁⲣⲛ̄ⲥⲱⲧⲙ̄	ⲙ̄ⲡⲣ̄ⲧⲣⲉⲛⲥⲱⲧⲙ̄
2	______	______
3	ⲙⲁⲣⲟⲩⲥⲱⲧⲙ̄	ⲙ̄ⲡⲣ̄ⲧⲣⲉⲩⲥⲱⲧⲙ̄
	ⲙⲁⲣⲉ—ⲡⲣⲱⲙⲉ ⲥⲱⲧⲙ̄	ⲙ̄ⲡⲣ̄ⲧⲣⲉ—ⲡⲣⲱⲙⲉ ⲥⲱⲧⲙ̄

[12] The negative of the injunctive consists of the negative imperative prefix ⲙ̄ⲡⲣ̄— and the appropriate form of the inflected infinitive.

Subordinate Clause Conjugations

Temporal

	Singular	Plural
1	ⲛ̄ⲧⲉⲣⲓⲥⲱⲧⲙ̄	ⲛ̄ⲧⲉⲣⲉⲛⲥⲱⲧⲙ̄[14]
2m	ⲛ̄ⲧⲉⲣⲉⲕⲥⲱⲧⲙ̄	ⲛ̄ⲧⲉⲣⲉⲧⲛ̄ⲥⲱⲧⲙ̄
2f	ⲛ̄ⲧⲉⲣⲉⲥⲱⲧⲙ̄[13]	
3m	ⲛ̄ⲧⲉⲣⲉϥⲥⲱⲧⲙ̄	ⲛ̄ⲧⲉⲣⲟⲩⲥⲱⲧⲙ̄
3f	ⲛ̄ⲧⲉⲣⲉⲥⲥⲱⲧⲙ̄	

ⲛ̄ⲧⲉⲣⲉ—ⲧⲉⲥϩⲓⲙⲉ ⲥⲱⲧⲙ̄

Conditional[15]

	Singular	Plural
1	ⲉⲓϣⲁⲛⲥⲱⲧⲙ̄	ⲉⲛϣⲁⲛⲥⲱⲧⲙ̄
2m	ⲉⲕϣⲁⲛⲥⲱⲧⲙ̄	ⲉⲧⲉⲧⲛ̄ϣⲁⲛⲥⲱⲧⲙ̄
2f	ⲉⲣⲉϣⲁⲛⲥⲱⲧⲙ̄[16]	
3m	ⲉϥϣⲁⲛⲥⲱⲧⲙ̄	ⲉⲩϣⲁⲛⲥⲱⲧⲙ̄
3f	ⲉⲥϣⲁⲛⲥⲱⲧⲙ̄	

ⲉⲣϣⲁⲛ—ⲧⲉⲥϩⲓⲙⲉ ⲥⲱⲧⲙ̄

"Until"

	Singular	Plural
1	ϣⲁⲛϯⲥⲱⲧⲙ̄	ϣⲁⲛⲧⲛ̄ⲥⲱⲧⲙ̄
2m	ϣⲁⲛⲧⲕ̄ⲥⲱⲧⲙ̄	ϣⲁⲛⲧⲉⲧⲛ̄ⲥⲱⲧⲙ̄
2f	ϣⲁⲛⲧⲉⲥⲱⲧⲙ̄	
3m	ϣⲁⲛⲧϥ̄ⲥⲱⲧⲙ̄	ϣⲁⲛⲧⲟⲩⲥⲱⲧⲙ̄
3f	ϣⲁⲛⲧⲥ̄ⲥⲱⲧⲙ̄	

ϣⲁⲛⲧⲉ—ⲧⲉⲥϩⲓⲙⲉ ⲥⲱⲧⲙ̄

[13] Variant ⲛ̄ⲧⲉⲣⲉⲣⲥⲱⲧⲙ̄.

[14] Variant ⲛ̄ⲧⲉⲣⲛ̄ⲥⲱⲧⲙ̄.

[15] There is also a short form for some of these, but it is rare. It omits the —ϣⲁⲛ: ⲉⲓⲥⲱⲧⲙ̄, ⲉⲕⲥⲱⲧⲙ̄, ⲉⲣⲉⲥⲱⲧⲙ, ⲉϥⲥⲱⲧⲙ̄, ⲉⲥⲥⲱⲧⲙ, ⲉⲛⲥⲱⲧⲙ̄, ⲉⲧⲉⲧⲛ̄ⲥⲱⲧⲙ̄, ⲉⲩⲥⲱⲧⲙ̄.

[16] Variant ⲉⲣϣⲁⲛⲥⲱⲧⲙ̄.

Conjunctive

	Singular	Plural
1	(ⲛ̄)ⲧⲁⲥⲱⲧⲙ̄	ⲛ̄ⲧⲛ̄ⲥⲱⲧⲙ̄
2m	ⲛ̄ⲅⲥⲱⲧⲙ̄[17]	ⲛ̄ⲧⲉⲧⲛ̄ⲥⲱⲧⲙ̄
2f	ⲛ̄ⲧⲉⲥⲱⲧⲙ̄	
3m	ⲛ̄ϥⲥⲱⲧⲙ̄[17]	ⲛ̄ⲥⲉⲥⲱⲧⲙ̄
3f	ⲛ̄ⲥⲥⲱⲧⲙ̄[17]	

ⲛ̄ⲧⲉ—ⲧⲉⲥϩⲓⲙⲉ ⲥⲱⲧⲙ̄

Future Conjunctive of Result (*Finalis*)

	Singular	Plural
1	ⲧⲁⲣⲓⲥⲱⲧⲙ̄	ⲧⲁⲣⲛ̄ⲥⲱⲧⲙ̄
2m	ⲧⲁⲣⲉⲕⲥⲱⲧⲙ̄	ⲧⲁⲣⲉⲧⲛ̄ⲥⲱⲧⲙ̄
2f	ⲧⲁⲣⲉⲥⲱⲧⲙ̄	
3m	ⲧⲁⲣⲉϥⲥⲱⲧⲙ̄	ⲧⲁⲣⲟⲩⲥⲱⲧⲙ̄
3f	ⲧⲁⲣⲉⲥⲥⲱⲧⲙ̄	

ⲧⲁⲣⲉ—ⲧⲉⲥϩⲓⲙⲉ ⲥⲱⲧⲙ̄

Bipartite or Durative Pattern

First Present

	Singular	Plural
1	ϯⲥⲱⲧⲙ̄	ⲧⲛ̄ⲥⲱⲧⲙ̄
2m	ⲕⲥⲱⲧⲙ̄	ⲧⲉⲧⲛ̄ⲥⲱⲧⲙ̄
2f	ⲧⲉⲥⲱⲧⲙ̄[18]	
3m	ϥⲥⲱⲧⲙ̄	ⲥⲉⲥⲱⲧⲙ̄
3f	ⲥⲥⲱⲧⲙ̄	

ⲡⲣⲱⲙⲉ ⲥⲱⲧⲙ̄

Imperfect

	Singular	Plural
1	ⲛⲉⲓⲥⲱⲧⲙ̄	ⲛⲉⲛⲥⲱⲧⲙ̄
2m	ⲛⲉⲕⲥⲱⲧⲙ̄	ⲛⲉⲧⲉⲧⲛ̄ⲥⲱⲧⲙ̄
2f	ⲛⲉⲣⲉⲥⲱⲧⲙ̄	
3m	ⲛⲉϥⲥⲱⲧⲙ̄	ⲛⲉⲩⲥⲱⲧⲙ̄
3f	ⲛⲉⲥⲥⲱⲧⲙ̄	

ⲛⲉⲣⲉ—ⲡⲣⲱⲙⲉ ⲥⲱⲧⲙ̄

[17] The superlinear stroke may shift in the second masculine singular (ⲛⲅ̄ⲥⲱⲧⲙ) and in the third masculine and feminine singular (ⲛϥ̄ⲥⲱⲧⲙ̄ and ⲛⲥ̄ⲥⲱⲧⲙ̄) forms. The second masculine singular also appears as ⲛ̄ⲕⲥⲱⲧⲙ̄.

[18] Variant ⲧⲣ̄ⲥⲱⲧⲙ̄.

First Future

	Singular	Plural
1	ϯⲛⲁⲥⲱⲧⲙ̅	ⲧⲛ̅ⲛⲁⲥⲱⲧⲙ̅
2m	ⲕⲛⲁⲥⲱⲧⲙ̅	ⲧⲉⲧⲛ̅ⲛⲁⲥⲱⲧⲙ̅
2f	ⲧⲉⲛⲁⲥⲱⲧⲙ̅[19]	
3m	ϥⲛⲁⲥⲱⲧⲙ̅	ⲥⲉⲛⲁⲥⲱⲧⲙ̅
3f	ⲥⲛⲁⲥⲱⲧⲙ̅	

ⲡⲣⲱⲙⲉ ⲛⲁⲥⲱⲧⲙ̅

ANOMALOUS PATTERNS

Imperative

Positive	Negative
ⲥⲱⲧⲙ̅	ⲙ̅ⲡⲣ̅ⲥⲱⲧⲙ̅

Inflected Infinitive

	Singular	Plural
1	ⲧⲣⲁⲥⲱⲧⲙ̅	ⲧⲣⲉⲛⲥⲱⲧⲙ̅
2m	ⲧⲣⲉⲕⲥⲱⲧⲙ̅	ⲧⲣⲉⲧⲉⲧⲛ̅ⲥⲱⲧⲙ̅
2f	ⲧⲣⲉⲥⲱⲧⲙ̅	
3m	ⲧⲣⲉϥⲥⲱⲧⲙ̅	ⲧⲣⲉⲩⲥⲱⲧⲙ̅
3f	ⲧⲣⲉⲥⲥⲱⲧⲙ̅	

ⲧⲣⲉ-ⲡⲣⲱⲙⲉ ⲥⲱⲧⲙ̅

[19] Variant ⲧⲉⲣⲁⲥⲱⲧⲙ̅.

THE CONVERSION SYSTEM

Introductory Notes

1. Sentence conjugations (not subordinate clause conjugations) in the tripartite pattern, conjugations in the bipartite pattern, and non-verbal sentences may convert a conjugation from a main clause to a subordinate clause, to a past time, or to a clause that focuses on a specific element through four possible converters: the relative, the circumstantial, the preterit, and the second tense (or focalizing) converters.
2. The conversions have different functions in a sentence.
   a. Relative conversion either expands an antecedent by creating a subordinate clause or functions much like an adjective by expanding a definite noun.
   b. Circumstantial conversion creates a subordinate clause that modifies another clause or term. Like a relative clause it may expand an antecedent, only the antecedent must be indefinitive (the relative is used why the antecedent is definite).
   c. Preterit conversion creates a past tense and may form an independent clause or sentence.
   d. Second tense or focalizing conversion indicates that the sentence has a special point of emphasis (i.e., a focal point). Like the preterit converters, second tense or focalizing converters may form an independent clause or sentence.
3. Some conversions have conversions of their own, i.e., conversions in the second degree or second stage conversions or even third degree conversions. I have placed these second degree conversions directly after the base conjugations which they convert.
4. There are two types of converters: some forms are fixed (i.e., they stand alone and do not change) and others are variable (i.e., they have prenominal and prepronominal forms). The two types of converters are not interchangeable, i.e., a variable converter cannot be substituted for a fixed converter or vice versa. There are separate lists of converters below for the tripartite pattern, bipartite pattern, and non-verbal sentences.
5. Where a form (in either the positive or negative version of the conjugation base for the tripartite pattern) is not attested, I have not attempted to supply one (I have followed the lists of conversions in Layton for attested forms). I have marked the spaces as blank (___).

TRIPARTITE OR NON-DURATIVE PATTERN

Converters

Conversion	Fixed Converters	Variable Converters	
		Prenominal	Prepronominal
Relative		ⲉⲛⲧⲁ—	ⲉⲛⲧ=
	ⲉⲧⲉ		
	ⲉ—		
Circumstantial	ⲉ—		
Preterit	ⲛⲉ—		
Second (Focalizing)		ⲛ̄ⲧⲁ—	ⲛ̄ⲧ=
	ⲉⲧⲉ		
	ⲉ—		

Converters by Tense

Tense	Relative	Circumstantial	Preterit	Second
First Perfect	ⲉⲛⲧⲁ—	ⲉ—	ⲛⲉ—	ⲛ̄ⲧⲁ—
	ⲛ̄ⲧⲁ—			ⲉⲛⲧⲁ—
Negative 1st Perfect	ⲉⲧⲉ	ⲉ—	ⲛⲉ—	ⲛ̄ⲧⲁ—
"Not Yet"	ⲉⲧⲉ	ⲉ—	ⲛⲉ—	___
Habitual	ⲉⲧⲉ	ⲉ—	ⲛⲉ—	ⲉ—
	ⲉ—			
Negative Habitual	ⲉⲧⲉ	ⲉ—	ⲛⲉ—	___
Third Future	___	ⲉ—	___	___
Negative 3rd Future	ⲉⲧⲉ	ⲉ—	___	___
Injunctive	___	___	___	___
Negative Injunctive	___	___	___	___

Conversions Illustrated

Converter	Positive	Negative
1 Perfect		
	ⲁϥⲥⲱⲧⲙ̄	ⲙ̄ⲡⲉϥⲥⲱⲧⲙ̄
Relative[20]	ⲉⲛⲧⲁϥⲥⲱⲧⲙ̄	ⲉⲧⲉ ⲙ̄ⲡⲉϥⲥⲱⲧⲙ̄
	ⲛ̄ⲧⲁϥⲥⲱⲧⲙ̄ (variant)	
	ⲉⲛⲧⲁ—ⲡⲣⲱⲙⲉ ⲥⲱⲧⲙ̄	ⲉⲧⲉ ⲙ̄ⲡⲉ—ⲡⲣⲱⲙⲉ ⲥⲱⲧⲙ̄
Circumstantial	ⲉ—ⲁϥⲥⲱⲧⲙ̄	ⲉ—ⲙ̄ⲡⲉϥⲥⲱⲧⲙ̄
		ⲙ̄ⲡⲉϥⲥⲱⲧⲙ̄ (vaiant)
	ⲉ—ⲡⲣⲱⲙⲉ ⲁϥⲥⲱⲧⲙ̄	ⲉ—ⲙ̄ⲡⲉ—ⲡⲣⲱⲙⲉ ⲥⲱⲧⲙ̄
Preterit	ⲛⲉ—ⲁϥⲥⲱⲧⲙ̄	ⲛⲉ—ⲙ̄ⲡⲉϥⲥⲱⲧⲙ̄
	ⲛⲉ—ⲡⲣⲱⲙⲉ ⲁϥⲥⲱⲧⲙ̄	ⲛⲉ—ⲡⲣⲱⲙⲉ ⲙ̄ⲡⲉϥⲥⲱⲧⲙ̄
Second	ⲛ̄ⲧⲁϥⲥⲱⲧⲙ̄	ⲛ̄ⲧⲁϥⲥⲱⲧⲙ̄ ⲁⲛ
	ⲉⲛⲧⲁϥⲥⲱⲧⲙ̄ (variant)	ⲉⲛⲧⲁϥⲥⲱⲧⲙ̄ ⲁⲛ (vaiant)
	ⲛ̄ⲧⲁ—ⲡⲣⲱⲙⲉ ⲥⲱⲧⲙ̄	ⲛ̄ⲧⲁ—ⲡⲣⲱⲙⲉ ⲥⲱⲧⲙ̄ ⲁⲛ
		ⲉⲧⲉ ⲙ̄ⲡϥ̄ⲥⲱⲧⲙ̄
2 Perfect (Secondary Conversion)		
	ⲛ̄ⲧⲁϥⲥⲱⲧⲙ̄	ⲛ̄ⲧⲁϥⲥⲱⲧⲙ̄ ⲁⲛ
Relative	———	———
Circumstantial	ⲉ—ⲛⲧⲁϥⲥⲱⲧⲙ̄	ⲉ—ⲛⲧⲁϥⲥⲱⲧⲙ̄ ⲁⲛ
Preterit	———	———
Second	———	———
"Not yet"		
		ⲙ̄ⲡⲁⲧϥ̄ⲥⲱⲧⲙ̄
Relative	———	ⲉⲧⲉ ⲙ̄ⲡⲁⲧϥ̄ⲥⲱⲧⲙ̄
		ⲉⲧⲉ ⲙ̄ⲡⲁⲧⲉ—ⲡⲣⲱⲙⲉ ⲥⲱⲧⲙ̄
Circumstantial	———	ⲉ—ⲙ̄ⲡⲁⲧϥ̄ⲥⲱⲧⲙ̄
		ⲙ̄ⲡⲁⲧϥ̄ⲥⲱⲧⲙ̄ (variant)
		ⲉ—ⲙ̄ⲡⲁⲧⲉ—ⲡⲣⲱⲙⲉ ⲥⲱⲧⲙ̄
Preterit	———	ⲛⲉ—ⲙ̄ⲡⲁⲧϥ̄ⲥⲱⲧⲙ̄
		ⲛⲉ-ⲙ̄ⲡⲁⲧⲉ—ⲡⲣⲱⲙⲉ ⲥⲱⲧⲙ̄
Second	———	———

[20] When the relative converter of the first perfect or other sentence conjugations in the tripartite pattern functions as the subject of the relative clause, the relative clause need only contain the first perfect relative converter and the infinitive, e.g., ⲡⲣⲱⲙⲉ ⲉⲛⲧⲁϥⲥⲱⲧⲙ̄ ("the man who heard"). When the relative converter is not the subject of the relative clause, the clause must contain a resumptive pronoun that specifies the syntactical function of the relative converter, e.g., ⲧⲉⲥϩⲓⲙⲉ ⲉⲛⲧⲁϥⲥⲱⲧⲙ̄ ⲉⲣⲟⲥ ("the woman whom he heard") or ⲉⲛⲧⲁ— ⲡⲣⲱⲙⲉ ⲥⲱⲧⲙ̄ ⲉⲣⲟⲥ (*whom* [feminine singular] the man heard). I have not supplied resumptive pronouns in the interest of space.

Converter	Positive	Negative
Habitual		
	ϣⲁϥⲥⲱⲧⲙ̄	ⲙⲉϥⲥⲱⲧⲙ̄
Relative	ⲉⲧⲉ ϣⲁϥⲥⲱⲧⲙ̄	ⲉⲧⲉ ⲙⲉϥⲥⲱⲧⲙ̄
	ⲉ—ϣⲁϥⲥⲱⲧⲙ̄	
	ⲉⲧⲉ ϣⲁⲣⲉ—ⲡⲣⲱⲙⲉ ⲥⲱⲧⲙ̄	ⲉⲧⲉ ⲙⲉⲣⲉ—ⲡⲣⲱⲙⲉ ⲥⲱⲧⲙ̄
Circumstantial	ⲉ—ϣⲁϥⲥⲱⲧⲙ̄	ⲉ—ⲙⲉϥⲥⲱⲧⲙ̄
	ⲉ—ϣⲁⲣⲉ—ⲡⲣⲱⲙⲉ ⲥⲱⲧⲙ̄	ⲉ—ⲙⲉⲣⲉ—ⲡⲣⲱⲙⲉ ⲥⲱⲧⲙ̄
Preterit	ⲛⲉ—ϣⲁϥⲥⲱⲧⲙ̄	ⲛⲉ—ⲙⲉϥⲥⲱⲧⲙ̄
	ⲛⲉ—ϣⲁⲣⲉ—ⲡⲣⲱⲙⲉ ⲥⲱⲧⲙ̄	ⲛⲉ—ⲙⲉⲣⲉ—ⲡⲣⲱⲙⲉ ⲥⲱⲧⲙ̄
Second	ⲉϣⲁϥⲥⲱⲧⲙ̄	———
	ⲉϣⲁⲣⲉ—ⲡⲣⲱⲙⲉ ⲥⲱⲧⲙ̄	
Third Future		
	ⲉϥⲉⲥⲱⲧⲙ̄	ⲛ̄ⲛⲉϥⲥⲱⲧⲙ̄
Relative	———	ⲉⲧⲉ ⲛ̄ⲛⲉϥⲥⲱⲧⲙ̄
		ⲉⲧⲉ ⲛ̄ⲛⲉ—ⲡⲣⲱⲙⲉ ⲥⲱⲧⲙ̄
Circumstantial	———	ⲉ—ⲛⲛⲉϥⲥⲱⲧⲙ̄
		ⲛ̄ⲛⲉϥⲥⲱⲧⲙ̄ (variant)
		ⲉ—ⲛ̄ⲛⲉ—ⲡⲣⲱⲙⲉ ⲥⲱⲧⲙ̄
Preterit	———	———
Second	———	———
Injunctive		
	ⲙⲁⲣⲉϥⲥⲱⲧⲙ̄	ⲙ̄ⲡⲣ̄ⲧⲣⲉϥⲥⲱⲧⲙ̄
Relative	———	———
Circumstantial	———	———
Preterit	———	———
Second	———	———

BIPARTITE OR DURATIVE PATTERN

Converters

Conversion	Fixed Converters	Variable Converters	
		Prenominal	Prepronominal
Relative		ⲉⲧⲉⲣⲉ—	ⲉⲧ=
	ⲉⲧ		
	ⲉⲧⲉ		
Circumstantial		ⲉⲣⲉ—	ⲉ=
	ⲉ—		
Preterit		ⲛⲉⲣⲉ—	ⲛⲉ=
Second (Focalizing)		ⲉⲣⲉ—	ⲉ=

Converters by Tense

Tense	Relative	Circumstantial	Preterit	Second
First Present	ⲉⲧⲉⲣⲉ/ⲉⲧ= ⲉⲧ	ⲉⲣⲉ/ⲉ=	ⲛⲉⲣⲉ/ⲛⲉ=	ⲉⲣⲉ/ⲉ=
Negative 1st Present	ⲉⲧⲉⲣⲉ/ⲉⲧ= ⲉⲧⲉ	ⲉⲣⲉ/ⲉ=	ⲛⲉⲣⲉ/ⲛⲉ=	ⲉⲣⲉ/ⲉ=
Imperfect	ⲉ or ⲉⲧⲉ	ⲉ	___	___
Negative Imperfect	ⲉ or ⲉⲧⲉ	ⲉ	___	___
Second Present	___	ⲉ	___	___
Negative 2nd Present	___	ⲉ	___	___
First Future	ⲉⲧⲉⲣⲉ/ⲉⲧ= ⲉⲧ	ⲉⲣⲉ/ⲉ=	ⲛⲉⲣⲉ/ⲛⲉ=	ⲉⲣⲉ/ⲉ=
Negative 1st Future	ⲉⲧⲉⲣⲉ/ⲉⲧ= ⲉⲧⲉ	ⲉⲣⲉ/ⲉ=	ⲛⲉⲣⲉ/ⲛⲉ=	ⲉⲣⲉ/ⲉ=

Conversions Illustrated

Converter	Positive	Negative[21]
1 Present		
	ⲥⲥⲱⲧⲙ̄	ⲛ̄ⲥⲥⲱⲧⲙ̄ ⲁⲛ
Relative[22]	ⲉⲧ ⲥⲱⲧⲙ̄	ⲉⲧⲉ ⲛⲥ̄ⲥⲱⲧⲙ̄ ⲁⲛ
	ⲉⲧⲥ̄ⲥⲱⲧⲙ̄	ⲉⲧⲉ ⲛ̄ⲥⲥⲱⲧⲙ̄ ⲁⲛ
	ⲉⲧⲉⲣⲉ— ⲧⲉⲥϩⲓⲙⲉ ⲥⲱⲧⲙ̄	ⲉⲧⲉⲣⲉ— ⲧⲉⲥϩⲓⲙⲉ ⲥⲱⲧⲙ̄ ⲁⲛ
Circumstantial	ⲉ—ⲥⲥⲱⲧⲙ̄	ⲉ—ⲛⲥ̄ⲥⲱⲧⲙ̄ ⲁⲛ
	ⲉⲣⲉ—ⲧⲉⲥϩⲓⲙⲉ ⲥⲱⲧⲙ̄	ⲉⲣⲉ—ⲧⲉⲥϩⲓⲙⲉ ⲥⲱⲧⲙ̄ ⲁⲛ
Preterit	ⲛⲉ—ⲥⲥⲱⲧⲙ̄	ⲛⲉ—ⲥⲥⲱⲧⲙ̄ ⲁⲛ
	ⲛⲉⲣⲉ—ⲧⲉⲥϩⲓⲙⲉ ⲥⲱⲧⲙ̄	ⲛⲉⲣⲉ—ⲧⲉⲥϩⲓⲙⲉ ⲥⲱⲧⲙ̄ ⲁⲛ
Second	ⲉⲥⲥⲱⲧⲙ̄	ⲛ̄ ⲉⲥⲥⲱⲧⲙ̄ ⲁⲛ
	ⲉⲣⲉ—ⲧⲉⲥϩⲓⲙⲉ ⲥⲱⲧⲙ̄	ⲉⲣⲉ—ⲧⲉⲥϩⲓⲙⲉ ⲥⲱⲧⲙ̄ ⲁⲛ
		ⲛ̄ ⲉⲣⲉ—ⲧⲉⲥϩⲓⲙⲉ ⲥⲱⲧⲙ̄ ⲁⲛ
Imperfect[23]		
	ⲛⲉⲥⲥⲱⲧⲙ̄ (ⲡⲉ)	ⲛⲉⲥⲥⲱⲧⲙ̄ ⲁⲛ (ⲡⲉ)
	ⲛⲉⲣⲉ—ⲧⲉⲥϩⲓⲙⲉ ⲥⲱⲧⲙ̄ (ⲡⲉ)	ⲛⲉⲣⲉ-ⲧⲉⲥϩⲓⲙⲉ ⲥⲱⲧⲙ̄ ⲁⲛ (ⲡⲉ)
Relative	ⲉ—ⲛⲉⲥⲥⲱⲧⲙ̄	ⲉ—ⲛⲉⲥⲥⲱⲧⲙ̄ ⲁⲛ
	ⲉⲧⲉ ⲛⲉⲥⲥⲱⲧⲙ̄	ⲉⲧⲉ ⲛⲉⲥⲥⲱⲧⲙ̄ ⲁⲛ
	ⲉⲧⲉ ⲛⲉⲣⲉ—ⲧⲉⲥϩⲓⲙⲉ ⲥⲱⲧⲙ̄	ⲉⲧⲉ ⲛⲉⲣⲉ-ⲧⲉⲥϩⲓⲙⲉ ⲥⲱⲧⲙ̄ ⲁⲛ

[21] The negatives of the first present are either ⲛ̄ ... ⲁⲛ or simply ⲁⲛ. Fixed converters normally use ⲛ̄ ... ⲁⲛ. The prenominal forms of the converters (ⲉⲧⲉⲣⲉ—, ⲉⲣⲉ—, ⲛⲉⲣⲉ—, ⲉⲣⲉ—) typically use only ⲁⲛ. The supralinear stroke over ⲛ̄ often shifts to the pronominal prefix in the second and third person singular forms, e.g., ⲛ̄ⲕⲥⲱⲧⲙ̄ ⲁⲛ or ⲛⲅ̄ⲥⲱⲧⲙ̄ ⲁⲛ.

[22] The relative converters for the first present are complex. The conjugation uses both fixed and variable forms of the converter. When the relative converter of the first present functions as the subject of the relative clause, the first present uses the fixed form of the converter ⲉⲧ, e.g., ⲧⲉⲥϩⲓⲙⲉ ⲉⲧ ⲥⲱⲧⲙ̄ ("the woman who listens"). When the relative clause negates the first present, the construction requires a different fixed form of the relative converter (ⲉⲧⲉ) and the repetition of the subject, e.g., ⲧⲉⲥϩⲓⲙⲉ ⲉⲧⲉ ⲛⲥ̄ⲥⲱⲧⲙ̄ ⲁⲛ ("the woman who is not listening"). When the relative converter is not the subject of the relative clause, the clause must contain a resumptive pronoun that specifies the syntactical function of the relative converter, e.g., ⲛ̄ϣⲁϫⲉ ⲉⲧⲥ̄ⲥⲱⲧⲙ̄ ⲉⲣⲟⲟⲩ ("the words that she hears"). When the relative clause negates the first present in such a construction, it uses ⲉⲧⲉ and a resumptive pronoun, e.g., ⲛ̄ϣⲁϫⲉ ⲉⲧⲉ ⲛⲥ̄ⲥⲱⲧⲙ̄ ⲉⲣⲟⲟⲩ ⲁⲛ ("the words that she is not hearing"). I have not supplied resumptive pronouns for the sake of space.

[23] The imperfect is a preterite conversion of the first present. It has its own conversions and may be considered a separate tense in the bipartite or durative pattern; however, its relation to the first present should be kept in mind.

Converter	Positive	Negative
Circumstantial	ⲉ—ⲛⲉⲥⲥⲱⲧⲙ̄	ⲉ—ⲛⲉⲥⲥⲱⲧⲙ̄ ⲁⲛ
	ⲉ—ⲛⲉⲣⲉ—ⲧⲉⲥϩⲓⲙⲉ ⲥⲱⲧⲙ̄	ⲉ—ⲛⲉⲣⲉ—ⲧⲉⲥϩⲓⲙⲉ ⲥⲱⲧⲙ̄ ⲁⲛ
Preterit	———	———
Second	———	———
2 Present (Secondary Conversion)		
	ⲉⲥⲥⲱⲧⲙ̄	ⲉⲥⲥⲱⲧⲙ̄ ⲁⲛ
Relative	———	———
Circumstantial	ⲉ—ⲉⲥⲥⲱⲧⲙ̄	ⲉ—ⲛ̄—ⲉⲥⲥⲱⲧⲙ̄ ⲁⲛ
	ⲉ—ⲉⲣⲉ—ⲧⲉⲥϩⲓⲙⲉ ⲥⲱⲧⲙ̄	ⲉ—ⲉⲣⲉ—ⲧⲉⲥϩⲓⲙⲉ ⲥⲱⲧⲙ̄ ⲁⲛ
Preterit	———	———
Second	———	———
1 Future		
	ⲥⲛⲁⲥⲱⲧⲙ̄	ⲛⲥ̄ⲛⲁⲥⲱⲧⲙ̄ ⲁⲛ
Relative[24]	ⲉⲧ ⲛⲁⲥⲱⲧⲙ̄	ⲛⲥ̄ⲛⲁⲥⲱⲧⲙ̄ ⲁⲛ
	ⲉⲧⲥ̄ⲛⲁⲥⲱⲧⲙ̄	ⲉⲧⲉ ⲛ̄ⲥⲛⲁⲥⲱⲧⲙ̄ ⲁⲛ
	ⲉⲧⲉⲣⲉ— ⲧⲉⲥϩⲓⲙⲉ ⲛⲁⲥⲱⲧⲙ̄	ⲉⲧⲉ ⲛ̄ ⲧⲉⲥϩⲓⲙⲉ ⲛⲁⲥⲱⲧⲙ̄ ⲁⲛ
Circumstantial	ⲉ—ⲥⲛⲁⲥⲱⲧⲙ̄	ⲉ—ⲛⲥ̄ⲛⲁⲥⲱⲧⲙ̄ ⲁⲛ
	ⲉⲣⲉ—ⲧⲉⲥϩⲓⲙⲉ ⲛⲁⲥⲱⲧⲙ̄	ⲉⲣⲉ—ⲧⲉⲥϩⲓⲙⲉ ⲛⲁⲥⲱⲧⲙ̄ ⲁⲛ
Preterit	ⲛⲉⲥⲛⲁⲥⲱⲧⲙ̄	ⲛⲉⲥⲛⲁⲥⲱⲧⲙ̄ ⲁⲛ
Preterit	ⲛⲉ—ⲛⲁⲥⲥⲱⲧⲙ̄	ⲛⲉ—ⲛⲁⲥⲥⲱⲧⲙ̄ ⲁⲛ
	ⲛⲉⲣⲉ—ⲧⲉⲥϩⲓⲙⲉ ⲛⲁⲥⲱⲧⲙ̄	ⲛⲉⲣⲉ—ⲧⲉⲥϩⲓⲙⲉ ⲛⲁⲥⲱⲧⲙ̄ ⲁⲛ
Second	ⲉⲥⲛⲁⲥⲱⲧⲙ̄	ⲉⲥⲛⲁⲥⲱⲧⲙ̄ ⲁⲛ
	ⲉⲣⲉ—ⲧⲉⲥϩⲓⲙⲉ ⲥⲱⲧⲙ̄	ⲉⲣⲉ—ⲧⲉⲥϩⲓⲙⲉ ⲛⲁⲥⲱⲧⲙ̄ ⲁⲛ
		ⲛ̄ ⲉⲣⲉ—ⲧⲉⲥϩⲓⲙⲉ ⲛⲁⲥⲱⲧⲙ̄ ⲁⲛ

[24] The relative converters for the first future are the same as for the first present. When the relative converter of the first future functions as the subject of the relative clause, the first future uses the fixed form of the converter ⲉⲧ, e.g., ⲧⲉⲥϩⲓⲙⲉ ⲉⲧ ⲛⲁⲥⲱⲧⲙ̄ ("the woman who will listen"). When the relative clause negates the first future, the construction requires a different fixed form of the relative converter (ⲉⲧⲉ) and the repetition of the subject, e.g., ⲧⲉⲥϩⲓⲙⲉ ⲉⲧⲉ ⲛⲥ̄ⲛⲁⲥⲱⲧⲙ̄ ⲁⲛ ("the woman who will not listen"). When the relative converter is not the subject of the relative clause, the clause must contain a resumptive pronoun that specifies the syntactical function of the relative converter, e.g., ⲛ̄ϣⲁϫⲉ ⲉⲧⲥ̄ⲛⲁⲥⲱⲧⲙ̄ ⲉⲣⲟⲟⲩ ("the words that she will hear"). When the relative clause negates the first future in such a construction, it uses ⲉⲧⲉ and a resumptive pronoun, e.g., ⲛ̄ϣⲁϫⲉ ⲉⲧⲉ ⲛⲥ̄ⲛⲁⲥⲱⲧⲙ̄ ⲉⲣⲟⲟⲩ ⲁⲛ ("the words that she will not hear").

NON-VERBAL CONVERSIONS

Converters

Conversion	Fixed Converters	Variable Converters	
		Prenominal	Prepronominal
Relative	ⲉⲧ		
	ⲉⲧⲉ		
Circumstantial		ⲉⲣⲉ—	ⲉ=
	ⲉ—		
Preterit	ⲛⲉ—		
Second (Focalizing)	ⲉ—		

Conversions Illustrated

Adverbial Predicate **(ⲡϫⲟⲉⲓⲥ ϩⲙ̄ ⲡⲏⲓ.)**

Converter	Positive	Negative
Relative	ⲡϫⲟⲉⲓⲥ ⲉⲧ ϩⲙ̄ ⲡⲏⲓ	ⲡϫⲟⲉⲓⲥ ⲉⲧⲉ ⲛ̄ϥ ϩⲙ̄ ⲡⲏⲓ ⲁⲛ
Circumstantial	ⲉ—ϥ ϩⲙ̄ ⲡⲏⲓ	ⲉ—(ⲛ̄)ϥ ϩⲙ̄ ⲡⲏⲓ ⲁⲛ
	ⲉⲣⲉ—ⲡϫⲟⲉⲓⲥ ϩⲙ̄ ⲡⲏⲓ	ⲉⲣⲉ—(ⲙ̄)ⲡϫⲟⲉⲓⲥ ϩⲙ̄ ⲡⲏⲓ ⲁⲛ
Preterit	ⲛⲉ—ϥ ϩⲙ̄ ⲡⲏⲓ (ⲡⲉ).	ⲛⲉ—ϥ ϩⲙ̄ ⲡⲏⲓ ⲁⲛ (ⲡⲉ).
	ⲛⲉⲣⲉ—ⲡϫⲟⲉⲓⲥ ϩⲙ̄ ⲡⲏⲓ.	ⲛⲉⲣⲉ—ⲡϫⲟⲉⲓⲥ ϩⲙ̄ ⲡⲏⲓ ⲁⲛ.
Second	ⲉ—ϥ ϩⲙ̄ ⲡⲏⲓ	ⲉ—ϥ ϩⲙ̄ ⲡⲏⲓ ⲁⲛ
	ⲉⲣⲉ—ⲡϫⲟⲉⲓⲥ ϩⲙ̄ ⲡⲏⲓ	ⲉⲣⲉ—(ⲙ̄)ⲡϫⲟⲉⲓⲥ ϩⲙ̄ ⲡⲏⲓ ⲁⲛ

Copulative or Nominal (ⲡⲉ, ⲧⲉ, ⲛⲉ)

Converter	Positive	Negative
Relative	ⲉⲧⲉ ⲟⲩϫⲟⲉⲓⲥ ⲧⲉ	ⲉⲧⲉ ⲛ̄ ⲟⲩϫⲟⲉⲓⲥ ⲁⲛ ⲧⲉ[25]
Circumstantial	ⲉ—ⲟⲩϫⲟⲉⲓⲥ ⲧⲉ	ⲉ—ⲛⲟⲩϫⲟⲉⲓⲥ ⲁⲛ ⲧⲉ
Preterit	ⲛⲉ—ⲟⲩϫⲟⲉⲓⲥ ⲧⲉ	ⲛⲉ ⲛ̄ ⲟⲩϫⲟⲉⲓⲥ ⲁⲛ ⲧⲉ

Existential and Possessive
(ⲟⲩⲛ̄—/ⲟⲩⲛ̄ⲧⲁ= and ⲙⲛ̄—/ⲙⲛ̄ⲧⲁ=)

Converter	Positive	Negative
Relative	ⲉⲧⲉ ⲟⲩⲛ̄—	ⲉⲧⲉ ⲙⲛ̄—
Circumstantial	ⲉ—ⲟⲩⲛ̄—	ⲉ—ⲙⲛ̄—
Preterit	ⲛⲉ—ⲟⲩⲛ̄—	ⲛⲉ—ⲙⲛ̄—
Second	ⲉ—ⲟⲩⲛ̄—	ⲉ—ⲙⲛ̄—

[25] ϫⲟⲉⲓⲥ is both m. and f. (*master* and *lady*).

INFLECTED PREDICATE ADJECTIVES

Converters

Conversion	Fixed Converters	Variable Converters	
		Prenominal	Prepronominal
Relative	ⲉⲧ		
Circumstantial	ⲉ—		
Preterit	ⲛⲉ—		
Second (Focalizing)	ⲉ—		

FULL PARADIGMS

Introductory Notes

1. The following pages offer the paradigms of the conjugations according to their placement in the Coptic verbal system.
2. Some conjugations have only a negative or only a positive form.

Tripartite or Non-Durative Pattern

Sentence or Main Clause Conjugations

First Perfect

	Positive	
	Singular	Plural
1	ⲁⲓⲥⲱⲧⲙ̅	ⲁⲛⲥⲱⲧⲙ̅
2m	ⲁⲕⲥⲱⲧⲙ̅	ⲁⲧⲉⲧⲛ̅ⲥⲱⲧⲙ̅
2f	ⲁⲣⲥⲱⲧⲙ̅[26]	
3m	ⲁϥⲥⲱⲧⲙ̅	ⲁⲩⲥⲱⲧⲙ̅
3f	ⲁⲥⲥⲱⲧⲙ̅	
	ⲁ—ⲧⲉⲥϩⲓⲙⲉ ⲥⲱⲧⲙ̅	

	Negative	
	Singular	Plural
1	ⲙ̅ⲡⲓⲥⲱⲧⲙ̅	ⲙ̅ⲡⲉⲛⲥⲱⲧⲙ̅
2m	ⲙ̅ⲡⲉⲕⲥⲱⲧⲙ̅	ⲙ̅ⲡⲉⲧⲛ̅ⲥⲱⲧⲙ̅
2f	ⲙ̅ⲡⲉⲥⲱⲧⲙ̅[27]	
3m	ⲙ̅ⲡⲉϥⲥⲱⲧⲙ̅	ⲙ̅ⲡⲟⲩⲥⲱⲧⲙ̅
3f	ⲙ̅ⲡⲉⲥⲥⲱⲧⲙ̅	
	ⲙ̅ⲡⲉ—ⲧⲉⲥϩⲓⲙⲉ ⲥⲱⲧⲙ̅	

Relative First Perfect

	Positive	
	Singular	Plural
1	ⲉⲛⲧⲁⲓⲥⲱⲧⲙ̅	ⲉⲛⲧⲁⲛⲥⲱⲧⲙ̅
2m	ⲉⲛⲧⲁⲕⲥⲱⲧⲙ̅	ⲉⲛⲧⲁⲧⲉⲧⲛ̅ⲥⲱⲧⲙ̅
2f	ⲉⲛⲧⲁⲣⲉⲥⲱⲧⲙ̅	
3m	ⲉⲛⲧⲁϥⲥⲱⲧⲙ̅	ⲉⲛⲧⲁⲩⲥⲱⲧⲙ̅
3f	ⲉⲛⲧⲁⲥⲥⲱⲧⲙ̅	
	ⲉⲛⲧⲁ—ⲧⲉⲥϩⲓⲙⲉ ⲥⲱⲧⲙ̅	

[26] Variant forms are ⲁⲥⲱⲧⲙ̅ and ⲁⲣⲉⲥⲱⲧⲙ̅.
[27] Variant ⲙ̅ⲡⲣ̅ⲥⲱⲧⲙ̅.

	Negative	
	Singular	Plural
1	ⲉⲧⲉ ⲙ̄ⲡⲓⲥⲱⲧⲙ̄	ⲉⲧⲉ ⲙ̄ⲡⲉⲛⲥⲱⲧⲙ̄
2m	ⲉⲧⲉ ⲙ̄ⲡⲉⲕⲥⲱⲧⲙ̄	ⲉⲧⲉ ⲙ̄ⲡⲉⲧⲛ̄ⲥⲱⲧⲙ̄
2f	ⲉⲧⲉ ⲙ̄ⲡⲉⲥⲱⲧⲙ̄	
3m	ⲉⲧⲉ ⲙ̄ⲡⲉϥⲥⲱⲧⲙ̄	ⲉⲧⲉ ⲙ̄ⲡⲟⲩⲥⲱⲧⲙ̄
3f	ⲉⲧⲉ ⲙ̄ⲡⲉⲥⲥⲱⲧⲙ̄	
	ⲉⲧⲉ ⲙ̄ⲡⲉ—ⲧⲉⲥϩⲓⲙⲉ ⲥⲱⲧⲙ̄	

Circumstantial First Perfect

	Positive	
	Singular	Plural
1	ⲉ—ⲁⲓⲥⲱⲧⲙ̄	ⲉ—ⲁⲛⲥⲱⲧⲙ̄
2m	ⲉ—ⲁⲕⲥⲱⲧⲙ̄	ⲉ—ⲁⲧⲉⲧⲛ̄ⲥⲱⲧⲙ̄
2f	ⲉ—ⲁⲣⲥⲱⲧⲙ̄	
3m	ⲉ—ⲁϥⲥⲱⲧⲙ̄	ⲉ—ⲁⲩⲥⲱⲧⲙ̄
3f	ⲉ—ⲁⲥⲥⲱⲧⲙ̄	
	ⲉ—ⲁ—ⲧⲉⲥϩⲓⲙⲉ ⲥⲱⲧⲙ̄	

	Negative	
	Singular	Plural
1	ⲉ—ⲙ̄ⲡⲓⲥⲱⲧⲙ̄	ⲉ—ⲙ̄ⲡⲉⲛⲥⲱⲧⲙ̄
2m	ⲉ—ⲙ̄ⲡⲉⲕⲥⲱⲧⲙ̄	ⲉ—ⲙ̄ⲡⲉⲧⲛ̄ⲥⲱⲧⲙ̄
2f	ⲉ—ⲙ̄ⲡⲉⲥⲱⲧⲙ̄	
3m	ⲉ—ⲙ̄ⲡⲉϥⲥⲱⲧⲙ̄	ⲉ—ⲙ̄ⲡⲟⲩⲥⲱⲧⲙ̄
3f	ⲉ—ⲙ̄ⲡⲉⲥⲥⲱⲧⲙ̄	
	ⲉ—ⲙ̄ⲡⲉ— ⲧⲉⲥϩⲓⲙⲉ ⲥⲱⲧⲙ̄	

Preterit First Perfect or Pluperfect

	Positive	
	Singular	Plural
1	ⲛⲉ—ⲁⲓⲥⲱⲧⲙ̄	ⲛⲉ—ⲁⲛⲥⲱⲧⲙ̄
2m	ⲛⲉ—ⲁⲕⲥⲱⲧⲙ̄	ⲛⲉ—ⲁⲧⲉⲧⲛ̄ⲥⲱⲧⲙ̄
2f	ⲛⲉ—ⲁⲣⲥⲱⲧⲙ̄	
3m	ⲛⲉ—ⲁϥⲥⲱⲧⲙ̄	ⲛⲉ—ⲁⲩⲥⲱⲧⲙ̄
3f	ⲛⲉ—ⲁⲥⲥⲱⲧⲙ̄	
	ⲛⲉ—ⲁ— ⲧⲉⲥϩⲓⲙⲉ ⲥⲱⲧⲙ̄	

	Negative	
	Singular	Plural
1	ⲛⲉ—ⲙ̄ⲡⲓⲥⲱⲧⲙ̄	ⲛⲉ—ⲙ̄ⲡⲉⲛⲥⲱⲧⲙ̄
2m	ⲛⲉ—ⲙ̄ⲡⲉⲕⲥⲱⲧⲙ̄	ⲛⲉ—ⲙ̄ⲡⲉⲧⲛ̄ⲥⲱⲧⲙ̄
2f	ⲛⲉ—ⲙ̄ⲡⲉⲥⲱⲧⲙ̄	
3m	ⲛⲉ—ⲙ̄ⲡⲉϥⲥⲱⲧⲙ̄	ⲛⲉ—ⲙ̄ⲡⲟⲩⲥⲱⲧⲙ̄
3f	ⲛⲉ—ⲙ̄ⲡⲉⲥⲥⲱⲧⲙ̄	
	ⲛⲉ—ⲙ̄ⲡⲉ— ⲧⲉⲥϩⲓⲙⲉ ⲥⲱⲧⲙ̄	

Second Perfect

	Positive	
	Singular	Plural
1	ⲛ̄ⲧⲁⲓⲥⲱⲧⲙ̄	ⲛ̄ⲧⲁⲛⲥⲱⲧⲙ̄
2m	ⲛ̄ⲧⲁⲕⲥⲱⲧⲙ̄	ⲛ̄ⲧⲁⲧⲉⲧⲛ̄ⲥⲱⲧⲙ̄
2f	ⲛ̄ⲧⲁⲣⲉⲥⲱⲧⲙ̄	
3m	ⲛ̄ⲧⲁϥⲥⲱⲧⲙ̄	ⲛ̄ⲧⲁⲩⲥⲱⲧⲙ̄
3f	ⲛ̄ⲧⲁⲥⲥⲱⲧⲙ̄	
	ⲛ̄ⲧⲁ— ⲧⲉⲥϩⲓⲙⲉ ⲥⲱⲧⲙ̄	

	Negative	
	Singular	Plural
1	ⲛ̄ⲧⲁⲓⲥⲱⲧⲙ̄ ⲁⲛ	ⲛ̄ⲧⲁⲛⲥⲱⲧⲙ̄ ⲁⲛ
2m	ⲛ̄ⲧⲁⲕⲥⲱⲧⲙ̄ ⲁⲛ	ⲛ̄ⲧⲁⲧⲉⲧⲛ̄ⲥⲱⲧⲙ̄ ⲁⲛ
2f	ⲛ̄ⲧⲁⲣⲉⲥⲱⲧⲙ̄ ⲁⲛ	
3m	ⲛ̄ⲧⲁϥⲥⲱⲧⲙ̄ ⲁⲛ	ⲛ̄ⲧⲁⲩⲥⲱⲧⲙ̄ ⲁⲛ
3f	ⲛ̄ⲧⲁⲥⲥⲱⲧⲙ̄ ⲁⲛ	
	ⲛ̄ⲧⲁ— ⲧⲉⲥϩⲓⲙⲉ ⲥⲱⲧⲙ̄ ⲁⲛ	

"Not Yet"

	Positive	
	Singular	Plural
	________	________

	Negative	
	Singular	Plural
1	ⲙ̄ⲡⲁϯⲥⲱⲧⲙ̄	ⲙ̄ⲡⲁⲧⲛ̄ⲥⲱⲧⲙ̄
2m	ⲙ̄ⲡⲁⲧⲕ̄ⲥⲱⲧⲙ̄	ⲙ̄ⲡⲁⲧⲉⲧⲛ̄ⲥⲱⲧⲙ̄
2f	ⲙ̄ⲡⲁⲧⲉⲥⲱⲧⲙ̄	
3m	ⲙ̄ⲡⲁⲧϥ̄ⲥⲱⲧⲙ̄	ⲙ̄ⲡⲁⲧⲟⲩⲥⲱⲧⲙ̄
3f	ⲙ̄ⲡⲁⲧⲥ̄ⲥⲱⲧⲙ̄	
	ⲙ̄ⲡⲁⲧⲉ—ⲧⲉⲥϩⲓⲙⲉ ⲥⲱⲧⲙ̄	

Relative "Not Yet"

	Positive	
	Singular	Plural
	———	———

	Negative	
	Singular	Plural
1	ⲉⲧⲉ ⲙ̄ⲡⲁϯⲥⲱⲧⲙ̄	ⲉⲧⲉ ⲙ̄ⲡⲁⲧⲛ̄ⲥⲱⲧⲙ̄
2m	ⲉⲧⲉ ⲙ̄ⲡⲁⲧⲕ̄ⲥⲱⲧⲙ̄	ⲉⲧⲉ ⲙ̄ⲡⲁⲧⲉⲧⲛ̄ⲥⲱⲧⲙ̄
2f	ⲉⲧⲉ ⲙ̄ⲡⲁⲧⲉⲥⲱⲧⲙ̄	
3m	ⲉⲧⲉ ⲙ̄ⲡⲁⲧϥ̄ⲥⲱⲧⲙ̄	ⲉⲧⲉ ⲙ̄ⲡⲁⲧⲟⲩⲥⲱⲧⲙ̄
3f	ⲉⲧⲉ ⲙ̄ⲡⲁⲧⲥ̄ⲥⲱⲧⲙ̄	

ⲉⲧⲉ ⲙ̄ⲡⲁⲧⲉ— ⲧⲉⲥϩⲓⲙⲉ ⲥⲱⲧⲙ̄

Circumstantial "Not Yet"

	Positive	
	Singular	Plural
	———	———

	Negative	
	Singular	Plural
1	ⲉ—ⲙⲡⲁϯⲥⲱⲧⲙ̄[30]	ⲉ—ⲙⲡⲁⲧⲛ̄ⲥⲱⲧⲙ̄
2m	ⲉ—ⲙⲡⲁⲧⲕ̄ⲥⲱⲧⲙ̄	ⲉ—ⲙⲡⲁⲧⲉⲧⲛ̄ⲥⲱⲧⲙ̄
2f	ⲉ—ⲙⲡⲁⲧⲉⲥⲱⲧⲙ̄	
3m	ⲉ—ⲙⲡⲁⲧϥ̄ⲥⲱⲧⲙ̄	ⲉ—ⲙⲡⲁⲧⲟⲩⲥⲱⲧⲙ̄
3f	ⲉ—ⲙⲡⲁⲧⲥ̄ⲥⲱⲧⲙ̄	

ⲉ—ⲙⲡⲁⲧⲉ— ⲧⲉⲥϩⲓⲙⲉ ⲥⲱⲧⲙ̄

Preterit "Not Yet"

	Positive	
	Singular	Plural
	———	———

	Negative	
	Singular	Plural
1	ⲛⲉ—ⲙ̄ⲡⲁϯⲥⲱⲧⲙ̄	ⲛⲉ—ⲙ̄ⲡⲁⲧⲛ̄ⲥⲱⲧⲙ̄
2m	ⲛⲉ—ⲙ̄ⲡⲁⲧⲕ̄ⲥⲱⲧⲙ̄	ⲛⲉ—ⲙ̄ⲡⲁⲧⲉⲧⲛ̄ⲥⲱⲧⲙ̄
2f	ⲛⲉ—ⲙ̄ⲡⲁⲧⲉⲥⲱⲧⲙ̄	
3m	ⲛⲉ—ⲙ̄ⲡⲁⲧϥ̄ⲥⲱⲧⲙ̄	ⲛⲉ—ⲙ̄ⲡⲁⲧⲟⲩⲥⲱⲧⲙ̄
3f	ⲛⲉ—ⲙ̄ⲡⲁⲧⲥ̄ⲥⲱⲧⲙ̄	

ⲛⲉ—ⲙ̄ⲡⲁⲧⲉ— ⲧⲉⲥϩⲓⲙⲉ ⲥⲱⲧⲙ̄

[30] This may also appear as ⲉ—ⲙ̄ⲡⲁϯⲥⲱⲧⲙ̄. While the superlinear stroke over the initial ⲙ̄ is unnecessary with a preceding ⲉ, it can ocour.

Habitual (*Praesens Consuetudinis*)[31]

	Positivc	
	Singular	Plural
1	ϣⲁⲓⲥⲱⲧⲙ̄	ϣⲁⲛⲥⲱⲧⲙ̄
2m	ϣⲁⲕⲥⲱⲧⲙ̄	ϣⲁⲧⲉⲧⲛ̄ⲥⲱⲧⲙ̄
2f	ϣⲁⲣ(ⲉ)ⲥⲱⲧⲙ̄	
3m	ϣⲁϥⲥⲱⲧⲙ̄	ϣⲁⲩⲥⲱⲧⲙ̄
3f	ϣⲁⲥⲥⲱⲧⲙ̄	
	ϣⲁⲣⲉ—ⲧⲉⲥϩⲓⲙⲉ ⲥⲱⲧⲙ̄	

	Negative	
	Singular	Plural
1	ⲙⲉⲓⲥⲱⲧⲙ̄	ⲙⲉⲛⲥⲱⲧⲙ̄
2m	ⲙⲉⲕⲥⲱⲧⲙ̄	ⲙⲉⲧⲉⲧⲛ̄ⲥⲱⲧⲙ̄
2f	ⲙⲉⲣⲉⲥⲱⲧⲙ̄	
3m	ⲙⲉϥⲥⲱⲧⲙ̄	ⲙⲉⲩⲥⲱⲧⲙ̄
3f	ⲙⲉⲥⲥⲱⲧⲙ̄	
	ⲙⲉⲣⲉ—ⲧⲉⲥϩⲓⲙⲉ ⲥⲱⲧⲙ̄	

Relative Habitual

	Positive[32]	
	Singular	Plural
1	ⲉⲧⲉ ϣⲁⲓⲥⲱⲧⲙ̄	ⲉⲧⲉ ϣⲁⲛⲥⲱⲧⲙ̄
2m	ⲉⲧⲉ ϣⲁⲕⲥⲱⲧⲙ̄	ⲉⲧⲉ ϣⲁⲧⲉⲧⲛ̄ⲥⲱⲧⲙ̄
2f	ⲉⲧⲉ ϣⲁⲣ(ⲉ)ⲥⲱⲧⲙ̄	
3m	ⲉⲧⲉ ϣⲁϥⲥⲱⲧⲙ̄	ⲉⲧⲉ ϣⲁⲩⲥⲱⲧⲙ̄
3f	ⲉⲧⲉ ϣⲁⲥⲥⲱⲧⲙ̄	
	ⲉⲧⲉ ϣⲁⲣⲉ— ⲧⲉⲥϩⲓⲙⲉ ⲥⲱⲧⲙ̄	

	Negative	
	Singular	Plural
1	ⲉⲧⲉ ⲙⲉⲓⲥⲱⲧⲙ̄	ⲉⲧⲉ ⲙⲉⲛⲥⲱⲧⲙ̄
2m	ⲉⲧⲉ ⲙⲉⲕⲥⲱⲧⲙ̄	ⲉⲧⲉ ⲙⲉⲧⲉⲧⲛ̄ⲥⲱⲧⲙ̄
2f	ⲉⲧⲉ ⲙⲉⲣⲉⲥⲱⲧⲙ̄	
3m	ⲉⲧⲉ ⲙⲉϥⲥⲱⲧⲙ̄	ⲉⲧⲉ ⲙⲉⲩⲥⲱⲧⲙ̄
3f	ⲉⲧⲉ ⲙⲉⲥⲥⲱⲧⲙ̄	
	ⲉⲧⲉ ⲙⲉⲣⲉ— ⲧⲉⲥϩⲓⲙⲉ ⲥⲱⲧⲙ̄	

[31] Some call this the aorist; however, this is misleading for anyone who is familiar with Greek.

[32] There is a variant form of the relative for the Habitual, ⲉ—.

Circumstantial Habitual

	Positive	
	Singular	Plural
1	ⲉ—ϣⲁⲓⲥⲱⲧⲙ̄	ⲉ—ϣⲁⲛⲥⲱⲧⲙ̄
2m	ⲉ—ϣⲁⲕⲥⲱⲧⲙ̄	ⲉ—ϣⲁⲧⲉⲧⲛ̄ⲥⲱⲧⲙ̄
2f	ⲉ—ϣⲁⲣ(ⲉ)ⲥⲱⲧⲙ̄	
3m	ⲉ—ϣⲁϥⲥⲱⲧⲙ̄	ⲉ—ϣⲁⲩⲥⲱⲧⲙ̄
3f	ⲉ—ϣⲁⲥⲥⲱⲧⲙ̄	
	ⲉ—ϣⲁⲣⲉ— ⲧⲉⲥϩⲓⲙⲉ ⲥⲱⲧⲙ̄	

	Negative	
	Singular	Plural
1	ⲉ—ⲙⲉⲓⲥⲱⲧⲙ̄	ⲉ—ⲙⲉⲛⲥⲱⲧⲙ̄
2m	ⲉ—ⲙⲉⲕⲥⲱⲧⲙ̄	ⲉ—ⲙⲉⲧⲉⲧⲛ̄ⲥⲱⲧⲙ̄
2f	ⲉ—ⲙⲉⲣⲉⲥⲱⲧⲙ̄	
3m	ⲉ—ⲙⲉϥⲥⲱⲧⲙ̄	ⲉ—ⲙⲉⲩⲥⲱⲧⲙ̄
3f	ⲉ—ⲙⲉⲥⲥⲱⲧⲙ̄	
	ⲉ—ⲙⲉⲣⲉ— ⲧⲉⲥϩⲓⲙⲉ ⲥⲱⲧⲙ̄	

Preterit Habitual

	Positive	
	Singular	Plural
1	ⲛⲉ—ϣⲁⲓⲥⲱⲧⲙ̄	ⲛⲉ—ϣⲁⲛⲥⲱⲧⲙ̄
2m	ⲛⲉ—ϣⲁⲕⲥⲱⲧⲙ̄	ⲛⲉ—ϣⲁⲧⲉⲧⲛ̄ⲥⲱⲧⲙ̄
2f	ⲛⲉ—ϣⲁⲣ(ⲉ)ⲥⲱⲧⲙ̄	
3m	ⲛⲉ—ϣⲁϥⲥⲱⲧⲙ̄	ⲛⲉ—ϣⲁⲩⲥⲱⲧⲙ̄
3f	ⲛⲉ—ϣⲁⲥⲥⲱⲧⲙ̄	
	ⲛⲉ—ϣⲁⲣⲉ—ⲧⲉⲥϩⲓⲙⲉ ⲥⲱⲧⲙ̄	

	Negative	
	Singular	Plural
1	ⲛⲉ—ⲙⲉⲓⲥⲱⲧⲙ̄	ⲛⲉ—ⲙⲉⲛⲥⲱⲧⲙ̄
2m	ⲛⲉ—ⲙⲉⲕⲥⲱⲧⲙ̄	ⲛⲉ—ⲙⲉⲧⲉⲧⲛ̄ⲥⲱⲧⲙ̄
2f	ⲛⲉ—ⲙⲉⲣⲉⲥⲱⲧⲙ̄	
3m	ⲛⲉ—ⲙⲉϥⲥⲱⲧⲙ̄	ⲛⲉ—ⲙⲉⲩⲥⲱⲧⲙ̄
3f	ⲛⲉ—ⲙⲉⲥⲥⲱⲧⲙ̄	
	ⲛⲉ—ⲙⲉⲣⲉ— ⲧⲉⲥϩⲓⲙⲉ ⲥⲱⲧⲙ̄	

Second Habitual

	Positive	
	Singular	Plural
1	ⲉϣⲁⲓⲥⲱⲧⲙ̄	ⲉϣⲁⲛⲥⲱⲧⲙ̄
2m	ⲉϣⲁⲕⲥⲱⲧⲙ̄	ⲉϣⲁⲧⲉⲧⲛ̄ⲥⲱⲧⲙ̄
2f	ⲉϣⲁⲣ(ⲉ)ⲥⲱⲧⲙ̄	
3m	ⲉϣⲁϥⲥⲱⲧⲙ̄	ⲉϣⲁⲩⲥⲱⲧⲙ̄
3f	ⲉϣⲁⲥⲥⲱⲧⲙ̄	
	ⲉ—ϣⲁⲣⲉ— ⲧⲉⲥϩⲓⲙⲉ ⲥⲱⲧⲙ̄	

	Negative	
	Singular	Plural
	———	———

Third Future

	Positive	
	Singular	Plural
1	ⲉⲓⲉⲥⲱⲧⲙ̄	ⲉⲛⲉⲥⲱⲧⲙ̄
2m	ⲉⲕⲉⲥⲱⲧⲙ̄	ⲉⲧⲉⲧⲛⲉⲥⲱⲧⲙ̄
2f	ⲉⲣⲉⲥⲱⲧⲙ̄	
3m	ⲉϥⲉⲥⲱⲧⲙ̄	ⲉⲩⲉⲥⲱⲧⲙ̄
3f	ⲉⲥⲉⲥⲱⲧⲙ̄	
	ⲉⲣⲉ—ⲧⲉⲥϩⲓⲙⲉ ⲥⲱⲧⲙ̄	

	Negative	
	Singular	Plural
1	ⲛ̄ⲛⲁⲥⲱⲧⲙ̄	ⲛ̄ⲛⲉⲛⲥⲱⲧⲙ̄
2m	ⲛ̄ⲛⲉⲕⲥⲱⲧⲙ̄	ⲛ̄ⲛⲉⲧⲛ̄ⲥⲱⲧⲙ̄
2f	ⲛ̄ⲛⲉⲥⲱⲧⲙ̄	
3m	ⲛ̄ⲛⲉϥⲥⲱⲧⲙ̄	ⲛ̄ⲛⲉⲩⲥⲱⲧⲙ̄
3f	ⲛ̄ⲛⲉⲥⲥⲱⲧⲙ̄	
	ⲛ̄ⲛⲉ—ⲧⲉⲥϩⲓⲙⲉ ⲥⲱⲧⲙ̄	

Relative Third Future

	Positive	
	Singular	Plural
	———	———

	Negative[33]	
	Singular	Plural
1	ⲉⲧⲉ ⲛ̄ⲛⲁⲥⲱⲧⲙ̄	ⲉⲧⲉ ⲛ̄ⲛⲉⲛⲥⲱⲧⲙ̄
2m	ⲉⲧⲉ ⲛ̄ⲛⲉⲕⲥⲱⲧⲙ̄	ⲉⲧⲉ ⲛ̄ⲛⲉⲧⲛ̄ⲥⲱⲧⲙ̄
2f	ⲉⲧⲉ ⲛ̄ⲛⲉⲥⲱⲧⲙ̄	
3m	ⲉⲧⲉ ⲛ̄ⲛⲉϥⲥⲱⲧⲙ̄	ⲉⲧⲉ ⲛ̄ⲛⲉⲩⲥⲱⲧⲙ̄
3f	ⲉⲧⲉ ⲛ̄ⲛⲉⲥⲥⲱⲧⲙ̄	
	ⲉⲧⲉ ⲛ̄ⲛⲉ— ⲧⲉⲥϩⲓⲙⲉ ⲥⲱⲧⲙ̄	

Circumstantial Third Future

	Positive	
	Singular	Plural
	________	________

	Negative[34]	
	Singular	Plural
1	ⲉ—ⲛ̄ⲛⲁⲥⲱⲧⲙ̄	ⲉ—ⲛ̄ⲛⲉⲛⲥⲱⲧⲙ̄
2m	ⲉ—ⲛ̄ⲛⲉⲕⲥⲱⲧⲙ̄	ⲉ—ⲛ̄ⲛⲉⲧⲛ̄ⲥⲱⲧⲙ̄
2f	ⲉ—ⲛ̄ⲛⲉⲥⲱⲧⲙ̄	
3m	ⲉ—ⲛ̄ⲛⲉϥⲥⲱⲧⲙ̄	ⲉ—ⲛ̄ⲛⲉⲩⲥⲱⲧⲙ̄
3f	ⲉ—ⲛ̄ⲛⲉⲥⲥⲱⲧⲙ̄	
	ⲉ—ⲛ̄ⲛⲉ— ⲧⲉⲥϩⲓⲙⲉ ⲥⲱⲧⲙ̄	

Injunctive (Causative Imperative or Optative)

	Positive	
	Singular	Plural
1	ⲙⲁⲣⲓⲥⲱⲧⲙ̄	ⲙⲁⲣⲛ̄ⲥⲱⲧⲙ̄
2m	________	________
2f	________	________
3m	ⲙⲁⲣⲉϥⲥⲱⲧⲙ̄	ⲙⲁⲣⲟⲩⲥⲱⲧⲙ̄
3f	ⲙⲁⲣⲉⲥⲥⲱⲧⲙ̄	
	ⲙⲁⲣⲉ—ⲧⲉⲥϩⲓⲙⲉ ⲥⲱⲧⲙ̄	

	Negative	
	Singular	Plural
1	ⲙ̄ⲡⲣ̄ⲧⲣⲁⲥⲱⲧⲙ̄	ⲙ̄ⲡⲣ̄ⲧⲣⲉⲛⲥⲱⲧⲙ̄
2m	________	________
2f	________	________
3m	ⲙ̄ⲡⲣ̄ⲧⲣⲉϥⲥⲱⲧⲙ̄	ⲙ̄ⲡⲣ̄ⲧⲣⲉⲩⲥⲱⲧⲙ̄
3f	ⲙ̄ⲡⲣ̄ⲧⲣⲉⲥⲥⲱⲧⲙ̄	
	ⲙ̄ⲡⲣ̄ⲧⲣⲉ—ⲧⲉⲥϩⲓⲙⲉ ⲥⲱⲧⲙ̄	

[33] There is a variant, ⲉⲧⲉ ⲛⲉ⸗.
[34] There are examples that lack the initial ⲉ—.

Clause or Subordinate Clause Conjugations

Temporal

	Positive	
	Singular	Plural
1	ⲛ̄ⲧⲉⲣⲓⲥⲱⲧⲙ̄	ⲛ̄ⲧⲉⲣⲛ̄ⲥⲱⲧⲙ̄[36]
2m	ⲛ̄ⲧⲉⲣⲉⲕⲥⲱⲧⲙ̄	ⲛ̄ⲧⲉⲣⲉⲧⲛ̄ⲥⲱⲧⲙ̄
2f	ⲛ̄ⲧⲉⲣⲉⲥⲱⲧⲙ̄[35]	
3m	ⲛ̄ⲧⲉⲣⲉϥⲥⲱⲧⲙ̄	ⲛ̄ⲧⲉⲣⲟⲩⲥⲱⲧⲙ̄
3f	ⲛ̄ⲧⲉⲣⲉⲥⲥⲱⲧⲙ̄	
	ⲛ̄ⲧⲉⲣⲉ—ⲧⲉⲥϩⲓⲙⲉ ⲥⲱⲧⲙ̄	

	Negative	
	Singular	Plural
1	ⲛ̄ⲧⲉⲣⲓⲧⲙ̄ⲥⲱⲧⲙ̄	ⲛ̄ⲧⲉⲣⲛ̄ⲧⲙ̄ⲥⲱⲧⲙ̄
2m	ⲛ̄ⲧⲉⲣⲉⲕⲧⲙ̄ⲥⲱⲧⲙ̄	ⲛ̄ⲧⲉⲣⲉⲧⲛ̄ⲧⲙ̄ⲥⲱⲧⲙ̄
2f	ⲛ̄ⲧⲉⲣⲉⲧⲙ̄ⲥⲱⲧⲙ̄	
3m	ⲛ̄ⲧⲉⲣⲉϥⲧⲙ̄ⲥⲱⲧⲙ̄	ⲛ̄ⲧⲉⲣⲟⲩⲧⲙ̄ⲥⲱⲧⲙ̄
3f	ⲛ̄ⲧⲉⲣⲉⲥⲧⲙ̄ⲥⲱⲧⲙ̄	
	ⲛ̄ⲧⲉⲣⲉⲧⲙ̄—ⲧⲉⲥϩⲓⲙⲉ ⲥⲱⲧⲙ̄	

Conditional

	Positive	
	Singular	Plural
1	ⲉⲓϣⲁⲛⲥⲱⲧⲙ̄	ⲉⲛϣⲁⲛⲥⲱⲧⲙ̄
2m	ⲉⲕϣⲁⲛⲥⲱⲧⲙ̄	ⲉⲧⲉⲧⲛ̄ϣⲁⲛⲥⲱⲧⲙ̄
2f	ⲉⲣⲉϣⲁⲛⲥⲱⲧⲙ̄[37]	
3m	ⲉϥϣⲁⲛⲥⲱⲧⲙ̄	ⲉⲩϣⲁⲛⲥⲱⲧⲙ̄
3f	ⲉⲥϣⲁⲛⲥⲱⲧⲙ̄	
	ⲉⲣϣⲁⲛ—ⲧⲉⲥϩⲓⲙⲉ ⲥⲱⲧⲙ̄	

	Negative[38]	
	Singular	Plural
1	ⲉⲓ(ϣⲁⲛ)ⲧⲙ̄ⲥⲱⲧⲙ̄	ⲉⲛ(ϣⲁⲛ)ⲧⲙ̄ⲥⲱⲧⲙ̄
2m	ⲉⲕ(ϣⲁⲛ)ⲧⲙ̄ⲥⲱⲧⲙ̄	ⲉⲧⲉⲧⲛ̄(ϣⲁⲛ)ⲧⲙ̄ⲥⲱⲧⲙ
2f	ⲉⲣⲉ(ϣⲁⲛ)ⲧⲙ̄ⲥⲱⲧⲙ̄	
3m	ⲉϥ(ϣⲁⲛ)ⲧⲙ̄ⲥⲱⲧⲙ̄	ⲉⲩ(ϣⲁⲛ)ⲧⲙ̄ⲥⲱⲧⲙ
3f	ⲉⲥ(ϣⲁⲛ)ⲧⲙ̄ⲥⲱⲧⲙ	
	ⲉⲣϣⲁⲛⲧⲙ̄— ⲧⲉⲥϩⲓⲙⲉ ⲥⲱⲧⲙ̄	
	ⲉⲣⲉⲧⲙ̄— ⲧⲉⲥϩⲓⲙⲉ ⲥⲱⲧⲙ̄	

35 Variant ⲛ̄ⲧⲉⲣⲉⲣⲥⲱⲧⲙ̄.
36 Variant ⲛ̄ⲧⲉⲣⲉⲛⲥⲱⲧⲙ̄.
37 Variant ⲉⲣϣⲁⲛⲥⲱⲧⲙ̄.
38 The shortened form is more common in the negative than the positive, e.g., ⲉⲓⲧⲙ̄ⲥⲱⲧⲙ̄.

“Until”

	Positive	
	Singular	Plural
1	ϣⲁⲛϯⲥⲱⲧⲙ̄	ϣⲁⲛⲧⲛ̄ⲥⲱⲧⲙ̄
2m	ϣⲁⲛⲧⲕ̄ⲥⲱⲧⲙ̄	ϣⲁⲛⲧⲉⲧⲛ̄ⲥⲱⲧⲙ̄
2f	ϣⲁⲛⲧⲉⲥⲱⲧⲙ̄	
3m	ϣⲁⲛⲧϥ̄ⲥⲱⲧⲙ̄	ϣⲁⲛⲧⲟⲩⲥⲱⲧⲙ̄
3f	ϣⲁⲛⲧⲥ̄ⲥⲱⲧⲙ̄	
	ϣⲁⲛⲧⲉ— ⲧⲉⲥϩⲓⲙⲉ ⲥⲱⲧⲙ̄	

	Negative	
	Singular	Plural
1	ϣⲁⲛϯⲧⲙ̄ⲥⲱⲧⲙ̄	ϣⲁⲛⲧⲛ̄ⲧⲙ̄ⲥⲱⲧⲙ̄
2m	ϣⲁⲛⲧⲕ̄ⲧⲙ̄ⲥⲱⲧⲙ̄	ϣⲁⲛⲧⲉⲧⲛ̄ⲧⲙ̄ⲥⲱⲧⲙ̄
2f	ϣⲁⲛⲧⲉⲧⲙ̄ⲥⲱⲧⲙ̄	
3m	ϣⲁⲛⲧϥ̄ⲧⲙ̄ⲥⲱⲧⲙ̄	ϣⲁⲛⲧⲟⲩⲧⲙ̄ⲥⲱⲧⲙ̄
3f	ϣⲁⲛⲧⲥ̄ⲧⲙ̄ⲥⲱⲧⲙ̄	
	ϣⲁⲛⲧⲉⲧⲙ̄— ⲧⲉⲥϩⲓⲙⲉ ⲥⲱⲧⲙ̄	

Conjunctive

	Positive	
	Singular	Plural
1	(ⲛ̄)ⲧⲁⲥⲱⲧⲙ̄	ⲛ̄ⲧⲛ̄ⲥⲱⲧⲙ̄
2m	ⲛⲅ̄ⲥⲱⲧⲙ̄[39]	ⲛ̄ⲧⲉⲧⲛ̄ⲥⲱⲧⲙ̄
2f	ⲛ̄ⲧⲉⲥⲱⲧⲙ̄	
3m	ⲛϥ̄ⲥⲱⲧⲙ̄[39]	ⲛ̄ⲥⲉⲥⲱⲧⲙ̄
3f	ⲛⲥ̄ⲥⲱⲧⲙ̄[39]	
	ⲛ̄ⲧⲉ— ⲧⲉⲥϩⲓⲙⲉ ⲥⲱⲧⲙ̄	

	Negative	
	Singular	Plural
1	(ⲛ̄)ⲧⲁⲧⲙ̄ⲥⲱⲧⲙ̄	ⲛ̄ⲧⲛ̄ⲧⲙ̄ⲥⲱⲧⲙ̄
2m	ⲛⲅ̄ⲧⲙ̄ⲥⲱⲧⲙ̄[39]	ⲛ̄ⲧⲉⲧⲛ̄ⲧⲙ̄ⲥⲱⲧⲙ̄
2f	ⲛ̄ⲧⲉⲧⲙ̄ⲥⲱⲧⲙ̄	
3m	ⲛϥ̄ⲧⲙ̄ⲥⲱⲧⲙ̄[39]	ⲛ̄ⲥⲉⲧⲙ̄ⲥⲱⲧⲙ̄
3f	ⲛⲥ̄ⲧⲙ̄ⲥⲱⲧⲙ̄[39]	
	ⲛ̄ⲧⲉⲧⲙ̄— ⲧⲉⲥϩⲓⲙⲉ ⲥⲱⲧⲙ̄	

[39] The superlinear stroke may also appear over the ⲛ̄ rather than shifting in the second masculine singular and third person singular forms, e.g., ⲛ̄ⲅⲥⲱⲧⲙ̄, ⲛ̄ϥⲥⲱⲧⲙ̄, and ⲛ̄ⲥⲥⲱⲧⲙ̄.

Future Conjunctive of Result (Finalis)

	Positive	
	Singular	Plural
1	ⲧⲁⲣⲓⲥⲱⲧⲙ̄	ⲧⲁⲣⲛ̄ⲥⲱⲧⲙ̄
2m	ⲧⲁⲣⲉⲕⲥⲱⲧⲙ̄	ⲧⲁⲣⲉⲧⲛ̄ⲥⲱⲧⲙ̄
2f	ⲧⲁⲣⲉⲥⲱⲧⲙ̄	
3m	ⲧⲁⲣⲉϥⲥⲱⲧⲙ̄	ⲧⲁⲣⲟⲩⲥⲱⲧⲙ̄
3f	ⲧⲁⲣⲉⲥⲥⲱⲧⲙ̄	
	ⲧⲁⲣⲉ— ⲧⲉⲥϩⲓⲙⲉ ⲥⲱⲧⲙ̄	

	Negative	
	Singular	Plural
	________	________

Bipartite or Durative Pattern

First Present

	Positive	
	Singular	Plural
1	ϯⲥⲱⲧⲙ̄	ⲧⲛ̄ⲥⲱⲧⲙ̄
2m	ⲕⲥⲱⲧⲙ̄	ⲧⲉⲧⲛ̄ⲥⲱⲧⲙ̄
2f	ⲧⲉⲥⲱⲧⲙ̄[40]	
3m	ϥⲥⲱⲧⲙ̄	ⲥⲉⲥⲱⲧⲙ̄
3f	ⲥⲥⲱⲧⲙ̄	
	ⲡⲣⲱⲙⲉ ⲥⲱⲧⲙ̄	
	ⲟⲩⲛ̄—ⲟⲩⲣⲱⲙⲉ ⲥⲱⲧⲙ̄	

	Negative	
	Singular	Plural
1	ⲛ̄ϯⲥⲱⲧⲙ̄ ⲁⲛ	ⲛ̄ⲧⲛ̄ⲥⲱⲧⲙ̄ ⲁⲛ
2m	ⲛⲅ̄ⲥⲱⲧⲙ̄ ⲁⲛ[41]	ⲛ̄ⲧⲉⲧⲛ̄ⲥⲱⲧⲙ̄ ⲁⲛ
2f	ⲛ̄ⲧⲉⲥⲱⲧⲙ̄ ⲁⲛ	
3m	ⲛϥ̄ⲥⲱⲧⲙ̄ ⲁⲛ[41]	ⲛ̄ⲥⲉⲥⲱⲧⲙ̄ ⲁⲛ
3f	ⲛⲥ̄ⲥⲱⲧⲙ̄ ⲁⲛ[41]	
	(ⲙ̄)ⲡⲣⲱⲙⲉ ⲥⲱⲧⲙ̄ ⲁⲛ	
	ⲙⲛ̄—ⲟⲩⲣⲱⲙⲉ ⲥⲱⲧⲙ̄	

[40] Variant ⲧⲣ̄ⲥⲱⲧⲙ̄.

[41] The superlinear stroke may also appear over the ⲛ̄ rather than shifting in the second masculine singular and third person singular forms.

Relative First Present

Relative Pronoun as the Subject of the Relative Clause
(Fixed Converter)

Positive	Negative
ⲉⲧ	ⲉⲧⲉ (ⲛ̅ ... ⲁⲛ)

Relative Pronoun that is not the Subject of the Relative Clause
(Variable Converter)

	Positive	
	Singular	Plural
1	ⲉϯⲥⲱⲧⲙ̅	ⲉⲧⲛ̅ⲥⲱⲧⲙ̅
2m	ⲉⲧⲕ̅ⲥⲱⲧⲙ̅	ⲉⲧⲉⲧⲛ̅ⲥⲱⲧⲙ̅
2f	ⲉⲧⲉ(ⲣ)ⲥⲱⲧⲙ̅	
3m	ⲉⲧϥ̅ⲥⲱⲧⲙ̅	ⲉⲧⲟⲩⲥⲱⲧⲙ̅
3f	ⲉⲧⲥ̅ⲥⲱⲧⲙ̅	
	ⲉⲧⲉⲣⲉ—ⲧⲉⲥϩⲓⲙⲉ ⲥⲱⲧⲙ̅	

	Negative	
	Singular	Plural
1	ⲉⲧⲉ ⲛ̅ϯⲥⲱⲧⲙ̅ ⲁⲛ	ⲉⲧⲉ ⲛ̅ⲧⲛ̅ⲥⲱⲧⲙ̅ ⲁⲛ
2m	ⲉⲧⲉ ⲛⲅ̅ⲥⲱⲧⲙ̅ ⲁⲛ[42]	ⲉⲧⲉ ⲛ̅ⲧⲉⲧⲛ̅ⲥⲱⲧⲙ̅ ⲁⲛ
2f	ⲉⲧⲉ ⲛ̅ⲧⲉⲥⲱⲧⲙ̅ ⲁⲛ	
3m	ⲉⲧⲉ ⲛϥ̅ⲥⲱⲧⲙ̅ ⲁⲛ[42]	ⲉⲧⲉ ⲛ̅ⲥⲉⲥⲱⲧⲙ̅ ⲁⲛ
3f	ⲉⲧⲉ ⲛⲥ̅ⲥⲱⲧⲙ̅ ⲁⲛ[42]	
	ⲉⲧⲉ—(ⲙ̅)ⲧⲉⲥϩⲓⲙⲉ ⲥⲱⲧⲙ̅ ⲁⲛ	

Circumstantial First Present

	Positive	
	Singular	Plural
1	ⲉⲓⲥⲱⲧⲙ̅	ⲉⲛⲥⲱⲧⲙ̅
2m	ⲉⲕⲥⲱⲧⲙ̅	ⲉⲧⲉⲧⲛ̅ⲥⲱⲧⲙ̅
2f	ⲉⲣ(ⲉ)ⲥⲱⲧⲙ̅	
3m	ⲉϥⲥⲱⲧⲙ̅	ⲉⲩⲥⲱⲧⲙ̅
3f	ⲉⲥⲥⲱⲧⲙ̅	
	ⲉⲣⲉ—ⲡⲣⲱⲙⲉ ⲥⲱⲧⲙ̅	

[42] The superlinear stroke may also appear over the ⲛ̅ rather than shifting in the second masculine singular and third person singular forms.

	Negative[43]	
	Singular	Plural
1	ⲉ—ⲛ̅ϯⲥⲱⲧⲙ̅ ⲁⲛ	ⲉ—ⲛ̅ⲧⲛ̅ⲥⲱⲧⲙ̅ ⲁⲛ
2m	ⲉ—ⲛⲅ̅ⲥⲱⲧⲙ̅ ⲁⲛ[44]	ⲉ—ⲛ̅ⲧⲉⲧⲛ̅ⲥⲱⲧⲙ̅ ⲁⲛ
2f	ⲉ—ⲛⲧⲉⲥⲱⲧⲙ̅ ⲁⲛ	
3m	ⲉ—ⲛϥ̅ⲥⲱⲧⲙ̅ ⲁⲛ[44]	ⲉ—ⲛ̅ⲥⲉⲥⲱⲧⲙ̅ ⲁⲛ
3f	ⲉ—ⲛⲥ̅ⲥⲱⲧⲙ̅ ⲁⲛ[44]	
	ⲉⲣⲉ—ⲡⲣⲱⲙⲉ ⲥⲱⲧⲙ̅ ⲁⲛ	

Preterit First Present

(=Imperfect)

	Positive	
	Singular	Plural
1	ⲛⲉⲓⲥⲱⲧⲙ̅ (ⲡⲉ)	ⲛⲉⲛⲥⲱⲧⲙ̅ (ⲡⲉ)
2m	ⲛⲉⲕⲥⲱⲧⲙ̅ (ⲡⲉ)	ⲛⲉⲧⲉⲧⲛ̅ⲥⲱⲧⲙ̅ (ⲡⲉ)
2f	ⲛⲉⲣⲉⲥⲱⲧⲙ̅ (ⲡⲉ)	
3m	ⲛⲉϥⲥⲱⲧⲙ̅ (ⲡⲉ)	ⲛⲉⲩⲥⲱⲧⲙ̅ (ⲡⲉ)
3f	ⲛⲉⲥⲥⲱⲧⲙ̅ (ⲡⲉ)	
	ⲛⲉⲣⲉ—ⲡⲣⲱⲙⲉ ⲥⲱⲧⲙ̅	
	ⲛⲉⲩⲛ̅ ⲟⲩⲣⲱⲙⲉ ⲥⲱⲧⲙ̅[45]	

	Negative	
	Singular	Plural
1	ⲛⲉⲓⲥⲱⲧⲙ̅ ⲁⲛ (ⲡⲉ)	ⲛⲉⲛⲥⲱⲧⲙ̅ ⲁⲛ (ⲡⲉ)
2m	ⲛⲉⲕⲥⲱⲧⲙ̅ ⲁⲛ (ⲡⲉ)	ⲛⲉⲧⲉⲧⲛ̅ⲥⲱⲧⲙ̅ ⲁⲛ (ⲡⲉ)
2f	ⲛⲉⲣⲉⲥⲱⲧⲙ̅ ⲁⲛ (ⲡⲉ)	
3m	ⲛⲉϥⲥⲱⲧⲙ̅ ⲁⲛ (ⲡⲉ)	ⲛⲉⲩⲥⲱⲧⲙ̅ ⲁⲛ (ⲡⲉ)
3f	ⲛⲉⲥⲥⲱⲧⲙ̅ ⲁⲛ (ⲡⲉ)	
	ⲛⲉⲣⲉ—ⲡⲣⲱⲙⲉ ⲥⲱⲧⲙ̅ ⲁⲛ (ⲡⲉ)	
	ⲛⲉ—ⲙⲛ̅ ⲟⲩⲣⲱⲙⲉ ⲥⲱⲧⲙ̅ (ⲡⲉ)	

[43] The superlinear stroke may disappear from the ⲛ̅ when it is preceded by an ⲉ—.

[44] The superlinear stroke may also stand over ⲛ̅ rather than shifting in the second masculine singular and third person singular forms.

[45] ⲛⲉⲩⲛ̅ is a contraction of ⲛⲉ—ⲟⲩⲛ̅.

Second Present

	Positive	
	Singular	Plural
1	ⲉⲓⲥⲱⲧⲙ̄	ⲉⲛⲥⲱⲧⲙ̄
2m	ⲉⲕⲥⲱⲧⲙ̄	ⲉⲧⲉⲧⲛ̄ⲥⲱⲧⲙ̄
2f	ⲉⲣ(ⲉ)ⲥⲱⲧⲙ̄	
3m	ⲉϥⲥⲱⲧⲙ̄	ⲉⲩⲥⲱⲧⲙ̄
3f	ⲉⲥⲥⲱⲧⲙ̄	
	ⲉⲣⲉ—ⲡⲣⲱⲙⲉ ⲥⲱⲧⲙ̄	

	Negative	
	Singular	Plural
1	ⲉⲓⲥⲱⲧⲙ̄ ⲁⲛ	ⲉⲛⲥⲱⲧⲙ̄ ⲁⲛ
2m	ⲉⲕⲥⲱⲧⲙ̄ ⲁⲛ	ⲉⲧⲉⲧⲛ̄ⲥⲱⲧⲙ̄ ⲁⲛ
2f	ⲉⲣ(ⲉ)ⲥⲱⲧⲙ̄ ⲁⲛ	
3m	ⲉϥⲥⲱⲧⲙ̄ ⲁⲛ	ⲉⲩⲥⲱⲧⲙ̄ ⲁⲛ
3f	ⲉⲥⲥⲱⲧⲙ̄ ⲁⲛ	
	ⲉⲣⲉ—ⲡⲣⲱⲙⲉ ⲥⲱⲧⲙ̄ ⲁⲛ	

Imperfect
(=Preterit First Present)

	Positive	
	Singular	Plural
1	ⲛⲉⲓⲥⲱⲧⲙ̄ (ⲡⲉ)	ⲛⲉⲛⲥⲱⲧⲙ̄ (ⲡⲉ)
2m	ⲛⲉⲕⲥⲱⲧⲙ̄ (ⲡⲉ)	ⲛⲉⲧⲉⲧⲛ̄ⲥⲱⲧⲙ̄ (ⲡⲉ)
2f	ⲛⲉⲣⲉⲥⲱⲧⲙ̄ (ⲡⲉ)	
3m	ⲛⲉϥⲥⲱⲧⲙ̄ (ⲡⲉ)	ⲛⲉⲩⲥⲱⲧⲙ̄ (ⲡⲉ)
3f	ⲛⲉⲥⲥⲱⲧⲙ̄ (ⲡⲉ)	
	ⲛⲉⲣⲉ—ⲡⲣⲱⲙⲉ ⲥⲱⲧⲙ̄	
	ⲛⲉⲩⲛ̄ ⲟⲩⲣⲱⲙⲉ ⲥⲱⲧⲙ̄[46]	

	Negative	
	Singular	Plural
1	ⲛⲉⲓⲥⲱⲧⲙ̄ ⲁⲛ (ⲡⲉ)	ⲛⲉⲛⲥⲱⲧⲙ̄ ⲁⲛ (ⲡⲉ)
2m	ⲛⲉⲕⲥⲱⲧⲙ̄ ⲁⲛ (ⲡⲉ)	ⲛⲉⲧⲉⲧⲛ̄ⲥⲱⲧⲙ̄ ⲁⲛ (ⲡⲉ)
2f	ⲛⲉⲣⲉⲥⲱⲧⲙ̄ ⲁⲛ (ⲡⲉ)	
3m	ⲛⲉϥⲥⲱⲧⲙ̄ ⲁⲛ (ⲡⲉ)	ⲛⲉⲩⲥⲱⲧⲙ̄ ⲁⲛ (ⲡⲉ)
3f	ⲛⲉⲥⲥⲱⲧⲙ̄ ⲁⲛ (ⲡⲉ)	
	ⲛⲉⲣⲉ—ⲡⲣⲱⲙⲉ ⲥⲱⲧⲙ̄ ⲁⲛ (ⲡⲉ)	
	ⲛⲉ—ⲙⲛ̄ ⲟⲩⲣⲱⲙⲉ ⲥⲱⲧⲙ̄ (ⲡⲉ)	

[35] ⲛⲉⲩⲛ̄ is a contraction of ⲛⲉ—ⲟⲩⲛ̄.

Relative Imperfect

	Positive	
	Singular	Plural
1	ⲉⲧⲉ ⲛⲉⲓⲥⲱⲧⲙ̄	ⲉⲧⲉ ⲛⲉⲛⲥⲱⲧⲙ̄
2m	ⲉⲧⲉ ⲛⲉⲕⲥⲱⲧⲙ̄	ⲉⲧⲉ ⲛⲉⲧⲉⲧⲛ̄ⲥⲱⲧⲙ̄
2f	ⲉⲧⲉ ⲛⲉⲣⲉⲥⲱⲧⲙ̄	
3m	ⲉⲧⲉ ⲛⲉϥⲥⲱⲧⲙ̄	ⲉⲧⲉ ⲛⲉⲩⲥⲱⲧⲙ̄
3f	ⲉⲧⲉ ⲛⲉⲥⲥⲱⲧⲙ̄	
	ⲉⲧⲉ ⲛⲉⲣⲉ—ⲡⲣⲱⲙⲉ ⲥⲱⲧⲙ̄	

	Negative	
	Singular	Plural
1	ⲉⲧⲉ ⲛⲉⲓⲥⲱⲧⲙ̄ ⲁⲛ	ⲉⲧⲉ ⲛⲉⲛⲥⲱⲧⲙ̄ ⲁⲛ
2m	ⲉⲧⲉ ⲛⲉⲕⲥⲱⲧⲙ̄ ⲁⲛ	ⲉⲧⲉ ⲛⲉⲧⲉⲧⲛ̄ⲥⲱⲧⲙ̄ ⲁⲛ
2f	ⲉⲧⲉ ⲛⲉⲣⲉⲥⲱⲧⲙ̄ ⲁⲛ	
3m	ⲉⲧⲉ ⲛⲉϥⲥⲱⲧⲙ̄ ⲁⲛ	ⲉⲧⲉ ⲛⲉⲩⲥⲱⲧⲙ̄ ⲁⲛ
3f	ⲉⲧⲉ ⲛⲉⲥⲥⲱⲧⲙ̄ ⲁⲛ	
	ⲉⲧⲉ ⲛⲉⲣⲉ—ⲡⲣⲱⲙⲉ ⲥⲱⲧⲙ̄ ⲁⲛ	

Alternate Relative Imperfect (Identical to Circumstantial)

	Positive	
	Singular	Plural
1	ⲉ—ⲛⲉⲓⲥⲱⲧⲙ̄	ⲉ—ⲛⲉⲛⲥⲱⲧⲙ̄
2m	ⲉ—ⲛⲉⲕⲥⲱⲧⲙ̄	ⲉ—ⲛⲉⲧⲉⲧⲛ̄ⲥⲱⲧⲙ̄
2f	ⲉ—ⲛⲉⲣⲉⲥⲱⲧⲙ̄	
3m	ⲉ—ⲛⲉϥⲥⲱⲧⲙ̄	ⲉ—ⲛⲉⲩⲥⲱⲧⲙ̄
3f	ⲉ—ⲛⲉⲥⲥⲱⲧⲙ̄	
	ⲉ—ⲛⲉⲣⲉ—ⲧⲉⲥϩⲓⲙⲉ ⲥⲱⲧⲙ̄	

	Negative	
	Singular	Plural
1	ⲉ—ⲛⲉⲓⲥⲱⲧⲙ̄ ⲁⲛ	ⲉ—ⲛⲉⲛⲥⲱⲧⲙ̄ ⲁⲛ
2m	ⲉ—ⲛⲉⲕⲥⲱⲧⲙ̄ ⲁⲛ	ⲉ—ⲛⲉⲧⲉⲧⲛ̄ⲥⲱⲧⲙ̄ ⲁⲛ
2f	ⲉ—ⲛⲉⲣⲉⲥⲱⲧⲙ̄ ⲁⲛ	
3m	ⲉ—ⲛⲉϥⲥⲱⲧⲙ̄ ⲁⲛ	ⲉ—ⲛⲉⲩⲥⲱⲧⲙ̄ ⲁⲛ
3f	ⲉ—ⲛⲉⲥⲥⲱⲧⲙ̄ ⲁⲛ	
	ⲉ—ⲛⲉⲣⲉ—ⲧⲉⲥϩⲓⲙⲉ ⲥⲱⲧⲙ̄ ⲁⲛ	

Circumstantial Imperfect

Positive

	Singular	Plural
1	ⲉ—ⲛⲉⲓⲥⲱⲧⲙ̅	ⲉ—ⲛⲉⲛⲥⲱⲧⲙ̅
2m	ⲉ—ⲛⲉⲕⲥⲱⲧⲙ̅	ⲉ—ⲛⲉⲧⲉⲧⲛ̅ⲥⲱⲧⲙ̅
2f	ⲉ—ⲛⲉⲣⲉⲥⲱⲧⲙ̅	
3m	ⲉ—ⲛⲉϥⲥⲱⲧⲙ̅	ⲉ—ⲛⲉⲩⲥⲱⲧⲙ̅
3f	ⲉ—ⲛⲉⲥⲥⲱⲧⲙ̅	
	ⲉ—ⲛⲉⲣⲉ—ⲡⲣⲱⲙⲉ ⲥⲱⲧⲙ̅	

Negative

	Singular	Plural
1	ⲉ—ⲛⲉⲓⲥⲱⲧⲙ̅ ⲁⲛ	ⲉ—ⲛⲉⲛⲥⲱⲧⲙ̅ ⲁⲛ
2m	ⲉ—ⲛⲉⲕⲥⲱⲧⲙ̅ ⲁⲛ	ⲉ—ⲛⲉⲧⲉⲧⲛ̅ⲥⲱⲧⲙ̅ ⲁⲛ
2f	ⲉ—ⲛⲉⲣⲉⲥⲱⲧⲙ̅ ⲁⲛ	
3m	ⲉ—ⲛⲉϥⲥⲱⲧⲙ̅ ⲁⲛ	ⲉ—ⲛⲉⲩⲥⲱⲧⲙ̅ ⲁⲛ
3f	ⲉ—ⲛⲉⲥⲥⲱⲧⲙ̅ ⲁⲛ	
	ⲉ—ⲛⲉⲣⲉ—ⲡⲣⲱⲙⲉ ⲥⲱⲧⲙ̅ ⲁⲛ	

First Future

Positive

	Singular	Plural
1	ϯⲛⲁⲥⲱⲧⲙ̅	ⲧⲛ̅ⲛⲁⲥⲱⲧⲙ̅
2m	ⲕⲛⲁⲥⲱⲧⲙ̅	ⲧⲉⲧⲛ̅ⲛⲁⲥⲱⲧⲙ̅
2f	ⲧⲉⲛⲁⲥⲱⲧⲙ̅[47]	
3m	ϥⲛⲁⲥⲱⲧⲙ̅	ⲥⲉⲛⲁⲥⲱⲧⲙ̅
3f	ⲥⲛⲁⲥⲱⲧⲙ̅	
	ⲡⲣⲱⲙⲉ ⲛⲁⲥⲱⲧⲙ̅	
	ⲟⲩⲛ̅—ⲟⲩⲣⲱⲙⲉ ⲛⲁⲥⲱⲧⲙ̅	

Negative

	Singular	Plural
1	ⲛ̅ϯⲛⲁⲥⲱⲧⲙ̅ ⲁⲛ	ⲛ̅ⲧⲛ̅ⲛⲁⲥⲱⲧⲙ̅ ⲁⲛ
2m	ⲛⲅ̅ⲛⲁⲥⲱⲧⲙ̅ ⲁⲛ[48]	ⲛ̅ⲧⲉⲧⲛ̅ⲛⲁⲥⲱⲧⲙ̅ ⲁⲛ
2f	ⲛ̅ⲧⲉⲛⲁⲥⲱⲧⲙ̅ ⲁⲛ	
3m	ⲛϥ̅ⲛⲁⲥⲱⲧⲙ̅ ⲁⲛ[48]	ⲛ̅ⲥⲉⲛⲁⲥⲱⲧⲙ̅ ⲁⲛ
3f	ⲛⲥ̅ⲛⲁⲥⲱⲧⲙ̅ ⲁⲛ[48]	
	(ⲙ̅) ⲡⲣⲱⲙⲉ ⲛⲁⲥⲱⲧⲙ̅ ⲁⲛ	
	ⲙⲛ̅—ⲟⲩⲣⲱⲙⲉ ⲛⲁⲥⲱⲧⲙ̅	

[47] Variant ⲧⲉⲣⲁⲥⲱⲧⲙ̅.

[48] The superlinear stroke may also stand over ⲛ̅ rather than shifting in the second masculine singular and third person singular forms.

Relative First Future

Relative Pronoun as the Subject of the Relative Clause
(Fixed Converter)

Positive	Negative First Future
ⲉⲧ	ⲉⲧⲉ (ⲛ̅ ... ⲁⲛ)

Relative Pronoun that is not the Subject of the Relative Clause
(Variable Converter)

	Positive	
	Singular	Plural
1	ⲉϯⲛⲁⲥⲱⲧⲙ̅	ⲉⲧⲛ̅ⲛⲁⲥⲱⲧⲙ̅
2m	ⲉⲧⲕ̅ⲛⲁⲥⲱⲧⲙ̅	ⲉⲧⲉⲧⲛ̅ⲛⲁⲥⲱⲧⲙ̅
2f	ⲉⲧⲉ(ⲣ)ⲛⲁⲥⲱⲧⲙ̅	
3m	ⲉⲧϥ̅ⲛⲁⲥⲱⲧⲙ̅	ⲉⲧⲟⲩⲛⲁⲥⲱⲧⲙ̅
3f	ⲉⲧⲥ̅ⲛⲁⲥⲱⲧⲙ̅	
	ⲉⲧⲉⲣⲉ—ⲡⲣⲱⲙⲉ ⲛⲁⲥⲱⲧⲙ̅	

	Negative	
	Singular	Plural
1	ⲉⲧⲉ ⲛ̅ϯⲛⲁⲥⲱⲧⲙ̅ ⲁⲛ	ⲉⲧⲉ ⲛ̅ⲧⲛ̅ⲛⲁⲥⲱⲧⲙ̅ ⲁⲛ
2m	ⲉⲧⲉ ⲛⲅ̅ⲛⲁⲥⲱⲧⲙ̅ ⲁⲛ[49]	ⲉⲧⲉ ⲛ̅ⲧⲉⲧⲛ̅ⲛⲁⲥⲱⲧⲙ̅ ⲁⲛ
2f	ⲉⲧⲉ ⲛ̅ⲧⲉⲛⲁⲥⲱⲧⲙ̅ ⲁⲛ	
3m	ⲉⲧⲉ ⲛϥ̅ⲛⲁⲥⲱⲧⲙ̅ ⲁⲛ[49]	ⲉⲧⲉ ⲛ̅ⲥⲉⲛⲁⲥⲱⲧⲙ̅ ⲁⲛ
3f	ⲉⲧⲉ ⲛⲥ̅ⲛⲁⲥⲱⲧⲙ̅ ⲁⲛ[49]	
	ⲉⲧⲉ (ⲙ̅)ⲡⲣⲱⲙⲉ ⲛⲁⲥⲱⲧⲙ̅ ⲁⲛ	

Circumstantial First Future

	Positive	
	Singular	Plural
1	ⲉⲓⲛⲁⲥⲱⲧⲙ̅	ⲉⲛⲛⲁⲥⲱⲧⲙ̅
2m	ⲉⲕⲛⲁⲥⲱⲧⲙ̅	ⲉⲧⲉⲧⲛ̅ⲛⲁⲥⲱⲧⲙ̅
2f	ⲉⲣⲉⲛⲁⲥⲱⲧⲙ̅	
3m	ⲉϥⲛⲁⲥⲱⲧⲙ̅	ⲉⲩⲛⲁⲥⲱⲧⲙ̅
3f	ⲉⲥⲛⲁⲥⲱⲧⲙ̅	
	ⲉⲣⲉ—ⲡⲣⲱⲙⲉ ⲛⲁⲥⲱⲧⲙ̅	

[49] The superlinear stroke may also stand over ⲛ̅ rather than shifting in the second masculine singular and third person singular forms.

	Negative[50]	
	Singular	Plural
1	ⲉ—ⲛ̄ϯⲛⲁⲥⲱⲧⲙ̄ ⲁⲛ	ⲉ—ⲛ̄ⲧⲛ̄ⲛⲁⲥⲱⲧⲙ̄ ⲁⲛ
2m	ⲉ—ⲛⲅ̄ⲥⲱⲧⲙ̄ ⲁⲛ[51]	ⲉ—ⲛ̄ⲧⲉⲧⲛ̄ⲛⲁⲥⲱⲧⲙ̄ ⲁⲛ
2f	ⲉ—ⲛ̄ⲧⲉⲛⲁⲥⲱⲧⲙ̄ ⲁⲛ	
3m	ⲉ—ⲛϥ̄ⲛⲁⲥⲱⲧⲙ̄ ⲁⲛ[51]	ⲉ—ⲛ̄ⲥⲉⲛⲁⲥⲱⲧⲙ̄ ⲁⲛ
3f	ⲉ—ⲛⲥ̄ⲛⲁⲥⲱⲧⲙ̄ ⲁⲛ[51]	
	ⲉⲣⲉ—(ⲙ̄)ⲡⲣⲱⲙⲉ ⲛⲁⲥⲱⲧⲙ̄ ⲁⲛ	

Preterit First Future

Imperfectum Futuri (Imperfect of Future)

	Positive	
	Singular	Plural
1	ⲛⲉⲓⲛⲁⲥⲱⲧⲙ̄	ⲛⲉⲛⲛⲁⲥⲱⲧⲙ̄
2m	ⲛⲉⲕⲛⲁⲥⲱⲧⲙ̄	ⲛⲉⲧⲉⲧⲛ̄ⲛⲁⲥⲱⲧⲙ̄
2f	ⲛⲉⲣⲉⲛⲁⲥⲱⲧⲙ̄	
3m	ⲛⲉϥⲛⲁⲥⲱⲧⲙ̄	ⲛⲉⲩⲛⲁⲥⲱⲧⲙ̄
3f	ⲛⲉⲥⲛⲁⲥⲱⲧⲙ̄	
	ⲛⲉⲣⲉ—ⲡⲣⲱⲙⲉ ⲛⲁⲥⲱⲧⲙ̄	

	Negative	
	Singular	Plural
1	ⲛⲉⲓⲛⲁⲥⲱⲧⲙ̄ ⲁⲛ	ⲛⲉⲛⲛⲁⲥⲱⲧⲙ̄ ⲁⲛ
2m	ⲛⲉⲕⲛⲁⲥⲱⲧⲙ̄ ⲁⲛ	ⲛⲉⲧⲉⲧⲛ̄ⲛⲁⲥⲱⲧⲙ̄ ⲁⲛ
2f	ⲛⲉⲣⲉⲛⲁⲥⲱⲧⲙ̄ ⲁⲛ	
3m	ⲛⲉϥⲛⲁⲥⲱⲧⲙ̄ ⲁⲛ	ⲛⲉⲩⲛⲁⲥⲱⲧⲙ̄ ⲁⲛ
3f	ⲛⲉⲥⲛⲁⲥⲱⲧⲙ̄ ⲁⲛ	
	ⲛⲉⲣⲉ—ⲡⲣⲱⲙⲉ ⲛⲁⲥⲱⲧⲙ̄ ⲁⲛ	

Second Future

	Positive	
	Singular	Plural
1	ⲉⲓⲛⲁⲥⲱⲧⲙ̄	ⲉⲛⲛⲁⲥⲱⲧⲙ̄
2m	ⲉⲕⲛⲁⲥⲱⲧⲙ̄	ⲉⲧⲉⲧⲛ̄ⲛⲁⲥⲱⲧⲙ̄
2f	ⲉⲣⲉⲛⲁⲥⲱⲧⲙ̄	
3m	ⲉϥⲛⲁⲥⲱⲧⲙ̄	ⲉⲩⲛⲁⲥⲱⲧⲙ̄
3f	ⲉⲥⲛⲁⲥⲱⲧⲙ̄	
	ⲉⲣⲉ—ⲡⲣⲱⲙⲉ ⲛⲁⲥⲱⲧⲙ̄	

[50] The superlinear stroke may disappear from the ⲛ̄ when it is preceded by an ⲉ—.

[51] The superlinear stroke may also stand over ⲛ̄ rather than shifting in the second masculine singular and third person singular forms.

	Negative	
	Singular	Plural
1	ⲉⲓⲛⲁⲥⲱⲧⲙ̅ ⲁⲛ	ⲉⲛⲛⲁⲥⲱⲧⲙ̅ ⲁⲛ
2m	ⲉⲕⲛⲁⲥⲱⲧⲙ̅ ⲁⲛ	ⲉⲧⲉⲧⲛ̅ⲛⲁⲥⲱⲧⲙ̅ ⲁⲛ
2f	ⲉⲣⲉⲛⲁⲥⲱⲧⲙ̅ ⲁⲛ	
3m	ⲉϥⲛⲁⲥⲱⲧⲙ̅ ⲁⲛ	ⲉⲩⲛⲁⲥⲱⲧⲙ̅ ⲁⲛ
3f	ⲉⲥⲛⲁⲥⲱⲧⲙ̅ ⲁⲛ	
	ⲉⲣⲉ—ⲡⲣⲱⲙⲉ ⲛⲁⲥⲱⲧⲙ̅ ⲁⲛ	

Anomalous Patterns

Imperative

Standard Imperative

Positive	Negative
ⲥⲱⲧⲙ̅	ⲙ̅ⲡⲣ̅ⲥⲱⲧⲙ̅

NOTES:

1. The imperative typically uses the infinitive without any indication of person or number. The infinitive may be in the absolute, prenominal, or prepronominal state, ⲥⲱⲧⲡ̅ ("choose"), ⲥⲉⲧⲡ—ⲙ̅ⲙⲟⲥ ("choose her"), ⲥⲟⲧⲡϥ̅ ("choose him").
2. The negative uses the prefix ⲙ̅ⲡⲣ̅—.

Special Imperative Forms

(Generally with ⲁ — Prefix)

Infinitive	Imperative	Prenominal Imperative	Prepronominal Imperative	Meaning
____	____	ⲁⲩ—	ⲁⲩⲉⲓ=	give, bring
ⲉⲓ	ⲁⲙⲟⲩ	____	____	come
ⲉⲓⲛⲉ	ⲁⲛⲓⲛⲉ	ⲁⲛⲓ—	ⲁⲛⲓ=	bring
ⲉⲓⲣⲉ	ⲁⲣⲓⲣⲉ	ⲁⲣⲓ—	ⲁⲣⲓ=	do
ⲗⲟ	____	____	ⲁⲗⲟ= (reflexive)	cease
____	ⲙⲟ	____	____	take
ⲛⲁⲩ	ⲁⲛⲁⲩ	____	____	look
ⲟⲩⲱⲛ	ⲁⲟⲩⲱⲛ	ⲟⲩⲛ̅—	____	open
ϫⲱ	____	ⲁϫⲓ—	ⲁϫⲓ=	say
ϯ	ϯ	ϯ— or ⲙⲁ—	ⲧⲁⲁ=	give

NOTES:

1. ⲁⲩ— also appears as ⲁⲩⲉ—, ⲁⲩⲉⲓⲥ—.

2. ⲉⲓ is unusual by having inflected forms in the imperative:
   2 m.s. ⲁⲙⲟⲩ
   2 f.s. ⲁⲙⲏ
   2 pl. ⲁⲙⲏⲉⲓⲧⲛ̄ or ⲁⲙⲏⲓⲧⲛ̄
3. ⲙⲟ has a distinct plural, ⲙ̄ⲙⲏⲉⲓⲧⲛ̄.

Injunctive

(Causative Imperative or Optative)[52]

	Positive	
	Singular	Plural
1	ⲙⲁⲣⲓⲥⲱⲧⲙ̄	ⲙⲁⲣⲛ̄ⲥⲱⲧⲙ̄
2m	(ⲥⲱⲧⲙ̄)[53]	(ⲥⲱⲧⲙ̄)[53]
2f	(ⲥⲱⲧⲙ̄)[53]	
3m	ⲙⲁⲣⲉϥⲥⲱⲧⲙ̄	ⲙⲁⲣⲟⲩⲥⲱⲧⲙ̄
3f	ⲙⲁⲣⲉⲥⲥⲱⲧⲙ̄	
	ⲙⲁⲣⲉ—ⲧⲉⲥϩⲓⲙⲉ ⲥⲱⲧⲙ̄	

	Negative	
	Singular	Plural
1	ⲙ̄ⲡⲣ̄ⲧⲣⲁⲥⲱⲧⲙ̄	ⲙ̄ⲡⲣ̄ⲧⲣⲉⲛⲥⲱⲧⲙ̄
2m	(ⲙ̄ⲡⲣ̄ⲥⲱⲧⲙ̄)	(ⲙ̄ⲡⲣ̄ⲥⲱⲧⲙ̄)
2f	(ⲙ̄ⲡⲣ̄ⲥⲱⲧⲙ̄)	
3m	ⲙ̄ⲡⲣ̄ⲧⲣⲉϥⲥⲱⲧⲙ̄	ⲙ̄ⲡⲣ̄ⲧⲣⲉⲩⲥⲱⲧⲙ̄
3f	ⲙ̄ⲡⲣ̄ⲧⲣⲉⲥⲥⲱⲧⲙ̄	
	ⲙ̄ⲡⲣ̄ⲧⲣⲉ—ⲧⲉⲥϩⲓⲙⲉ ⲥⲱⲧⲙ̄	

[52] The injunctive belongs to the sentence conjugation system of the tripartite pattern. It is repeated here as a reminder that it functions as a form of the imperative.

[53] The injunctive proper only includes the first and third persons; the second person forms of the imperative are included for the sake of completion. It is pedagogically useful to think of the imperative as the second person of the injunctive or the injunctive as the first and third person forms of the imperative.

INFLECTED OR CAUSATIVE INFINITIVE

INTRODUCTORY NOTES

1. The inflected infinitive has two forms.
   a. Like other verbal units, it may consist of the conjugation base marker, the subject, and the infinitive, e.g., ⲧⲣⲉⲥⲥⲱⲧⲙ̄ ("that she hear" in which ⲧⲣⲉ is the conjugation base marker, ⲥ the subject, and ⲥⲱⲧⲙ̄ the infinitive). In these cases, the infinitive serves as a complementary infinitive or in combination with a preposition in an adverbial infinitive phrase, e.g., ϯⲟⲩⲱϣ ⲉⲧⲣⲉⲕⲥⲱⲧⲙ̄ ⲉⲣⲟⲓ ("I want you to listen to me") or ⲙⲛ̄ⲛ̄ⲥⲁ ⲧⲣⲁⲥⲱⲧⲙ̄ ⲉⲣⲟϥ ("after I heard him").
   b. It may also be conjugated in both the tripartite and bipartite patterns, e.g., ⲁⲕⲧⲣⲉϥⲥⲱⲧⲙ̄ ⲉⲣⲟⲥ ("you caused him to listen to her") or ϯⲧⲣⲉⲥⲥⲱⲧⲙ̄ ⲉⲣⲟϥ ("I am making her listen to him"). In the first instance, the sequence of the grammar is conjugation base (ⲁ, first perfect), subject (ⲕ, "you"), inflected infinitive (ⲧⲣⲉ, "caused"), object of the first infinitive that functions as the subject of the next infinitive (ϥ ,"him"), second infinitive (ⲥⲱⲧⲙ̄, "to listen"), object of the second infinitive (ⲉⲣⲟⲥ, "to her").
2. Sometimes the infinitive is causative (hence the alternate name) and sometimes it is not. As a rule of thumb, students may consider it non-causative when it is a complementary infinitive ((ⲉ)ϣ— is an exception) and causative when it is conjugated.
3. The inflected infinitive is negated in different ways depending on the construction.
   a. When the inflected infinitive is not conjugated, the negative is determined by the construction:
      1.) It appears immediately after ⲉ– (as in a circumstantial conversion), e.g., ⲉ–ⲧⲙ̄–ⲧⲣⲉϥ ⲥⲱⲧⲙ̄ ("since he did not hear").
      2.) It appears after ⲧⲣⲉ– when it stands in a prepositional phrase, e.g., ϩⲙ̄ ⲡⲧⲣⲉϥ–ⲧⲙ̄–ⲥⲱⲧⲙ̄ ("while he was/is not listening").
   b. When the inflected infinitive is conjugated, the negative of the sentence conjugations is used.
   c. When the inflected infinitive follows the verbal auxiliary ⲛⲁ– in the first future, ⲧⲙ̄ stands between ⲧⲣⲉ– and the infinitive, e.g., ϯⲛⲁⲧⲙ̄ⲧⲣⲉϥⲥⲱⲧⲙ̄ ("I will not make him listen").
4. Inflected infinitives appear in the conversions of the conjugated infinitives. The conversions are not repeated below, but students should remember that an inflected infinitive may appear in conversions, e.g., a relative conversion of the first perfect or a circumstantial conversion of the first present.
5. In the examples below, I have used the third person pronominal element (sometimes ϥ and sometimes ⲥ and sometimes ⲉⲩ) for the inflected infinitive for the sake of simplicity.

The Simple Inflected Infinitive

	Positive	
	Singular	Plural
1	ⲧⲣⲁⲥⲱⲧⲙ̄	ⲧⲣⲉⲛⲥⲱⲧⲙ̄
2m	ⲧⲣⲉⲕⲥⲱⲧⲙ̄	ⲧⲣⲉⲧⲛ̄ⲥⲱⲧⲙ̄[54]
2f	ⲧⲣⲉⲥⲱⲧⲙ̄	
3m	ⲧⲣⲉϥⲥⲱⲧⲙ̄	ⲧⲣⲉⲩⲥⲱⲧⲙ̄
3f	ⲧⲣⲉⲥⲥⲱⲧⲙ̄	
	ⲧⲣⲉ—ⲡⲣⲱⲙⲉ ⲥⲱⲧⲙ̄	

	Negative[55]	
	Singular	Plural
1	ⲧⲣⲁⲧⲙ̄ⲥⲱⲧⲙ̄	ⲧⲣⲉⲛⲧⲙ̄ⲥⲱⲧⲙ̄
2m	ⲧⲣⲉⲕⲧⲙ̄ⲥⲱⲧⲙ̄	ⲧⲣⲉⲧⲉⲧⲛ̄ⲧⲙ̄ⲥⲱⲧⲙ̄
2f	ⲧⲣⲉⲧⲙ̄ⲥⲱⲧⲙ̄	
3m	ⲧⲣⲉϥⲧⲙ̄ⲥⲱⲧⲙ̄	ⲧⲣⲉⲩⲧⲙ̄ⲥⲱⲧⲙ̄
3f	ⲧⲣⲉⲥⲧⲙ̄ⲥⲱⲧⲙ̄	
	ⲧⲣⲉⲧⲙ̄—ⲡⲣⲱⲙⲉ ⲥⲱⲧⲙ̄	

The Conjugated Inflective Infinitive

The Tripartite or Non-Durative Pattern

Sentence Conjugations

First Perfect

	Positive	
	Singular	Plural
1	ⲁⲓⲧⲣⲉϥⲥⲱⲧⲙ̄	ⲁⲛⲧⲣⲉϥⲥⲱⲧⲙ̄
2m	ⲁⲕⲧⲣⲉϥⲥⲱⲧⲙ̄	ⲁⲧⲉⲧⲛ̄ⲧⲣⲉϥⲥⲱⲧⲙ̄
2f	ⲁⲣⲧⲣⲉϥⲥⲱⲧⲙ̄	
3m	ⲁϥⲧⲣⲉϥⲥⲱⲧⲙ̄	ⲁⲩⲧⲣⲉϥⲥⲱⲧⲙ̄
3f	ⲁⲥⲧⲣⲉϥⲥⲱⲧⲙ̄	
	ⲁⲥ—ⲧⲣⲉ—ⲡⲣⲱⲙⲉ ⲥⲱⲧⲙ̄	

[54] Variant ⲧⲣⲉⲧⲉⲧⲛ̄ⲥⲱⲧⲙ̄.

[55] The position of —ⲧⲙ̄— depends on the construction. See the introductory note 3.

Negative First Perfect

	Singular	Plural
1	ⲙ̅ⲡⲓⲧⲣⲉϥⲥⲱⲧⲙ̅	ⲙ̅ⲡⲉⲛⲧⲣⲉϥⲥⲱⲧⲙ̅
2m	ⲙ̅ⲡⲉⲕⲧⲣⲉϥⲥⲱⲧⲙ̅	ⲙ̅ⲡⲉⲧⲛ̅ⲧⲣⲉϥⲥⲱⲧⲙ̅
2f	ⲙ̅ⲡⲉⲧⲣⲉϥⲥⲱⲧⲙ̅	
3m	ⲙ̅ⲡⲉϥⲧⲣⲉϥⲥⲱⲧⲙ̅	ⲙ̅ⲡⲟⲩⲧⲣⲉϥⲥⲱⲧⲙ̅
3f	ⲙ̅ⲡⲉⲥⲧⲣⲉϥⲥⲱⲧⲙ̅	

ⲙ̅ⲡⲉⲥ—ⲧⲣⲉ—ⲡⲣⲱⲙⲉ ⲥⲱⲧⲙ̅

“Not Yet”

	Positive	
	Singular	Plural
	________	________

	Negative	
	Singular	Plural
1	ⲙ̅ⲡⲁϯⲧⲣⲉⲥⲥⲱⲧⲙ̅	ⲙ̅ⲡⲁⲧⲛ̅ⲧⲣⲉⲥⲥⲱⲧⲙ̅
2m	ⲙ̅ⲡⲁⲧⲕ̅ⲧⲣⲉⲥⲥⲱⲧⲙ̅	ⲙ̅ⲡⲁⲧⲉⲧⲛ̅ⲧⲣⲉⲥⲥⲱⲧⲙ̅
2f	ⲙ̅ⲡⲁⲧⲉⲧⲣⲉⲥⲥⲱⲧⲙ̅	
3m	ⲙ̅ⲡⲁⲧϥ̅ⲧⲣⲉⲥⲥⲱⲧⲙ̅	ⲙ̅ⲡⲁⲧⲟⲩⲧⲣⲉⲥⲥⲱⲧⲙ̅
3f	ⲙ̅ⲡⲁⲧⲥ̅ⲧⲣⲉⲥⲥⲱⲧⲙ̅	

ⲙ̅ⲡⲁⲧⲉϥ—ⲧⲣⲉ–ⲧⲉⲥϩⲓⲙⲉ ⲥⲱⲧⲙ̅

Habitual (*Praesens Consuetudinis*)[56]

	Positive	
	Singular	Plural
1	ϣⲁⲓⲧⲣⲉⲥⲥⲱⲧⲙ̅	ϣⲁⲛⲧⲣⲉⲥⲥⲱⲧⲙ̅
2m	ϣⲁⲕⲧⲣⲉⲥⲥⲱⲧⲙ̅	ϣⲁⲧⲉⲧⲛ̅ⲧⲣⲉⲥⲥⲱⲧⲙ̅
2f	ϣⲁⲣ(ⲉ)ⲧⲣⲉⲥⲥⲱⲧⲙ̅	
3m	ϣⲁϥⲧⲣⲉⲥⲥⲱⲧⲙ̅	ϣⲁⲩⲧⲣⲉⲥⲥⲱⲧⲙ̅
3f	ϣⲁⲥⲧⲣⲉⲥⲥⲱⲧⲙ̅	

ϣⲁⲣⲉϥ—ⲧⲣⲉ–ⲧⲉⲥϩⲓⲙⲉ ⲥⲱⲧⲙ̅

[56] Some call this the aorist; however, this can be misleading for anyone who is familiar with Greek.

	Negative	
	Singular	Plural
1	ⲙⲉⲓⲧⲣⲉⲥⲥⲱⲧⲙ̄	ⲙⲉⲛⲧⲣⲉⲥⲥⲱⲧⲙ̄
2m	ⲙⲉⲕⲧⲣⲉⲥⲥⲱⲧⲙ̄	ⲙⲉⲧⲉⲧⲛ̄ⲧⲣⲉⲥⲥⲱⲧⲙ̄
2f	ⲙⲉⲣⲉⲧⲣⲉⲥⲥⲱⲧⲙ̄	
3m	ⲙⲉϥⲧⲣⲉⲥⲥⲱⲧⲙ̄	ⲙⲉⲩⲧⲣⲉⲥⲥⲱⲧⲙ̄
3f	ⲙⲉⲥⲧⲣⲉⲥⲥⲱⲧⲙ̄	
	ⲙⲉⲣⲉϥ—ⲧⲣⲉ–ⲧⲉⲥϩⲓⲙⲉ ⲥⲱⲧⲙ̄	

Third Future

	Positive	
	Singular	Plural
1	ⲉⲓⲉⲧⲣⲉⲥⲥⲱⲧⲙ̄	ⲉⲛⲉⲧⲣⲉⲥⲥⲱⲧⲙ̄
2m	ⲉⲕⲉⲧⲣⲉⲥⲥⲱⲧⲙ̄	ⲉⲧⲉⲧⲛⲉⲧⲣⲉⲥⲥⲱⲧⲙ̄
2f	ⲉⲣⲉⲧⲣⲉⲥⲥⲱⲧⲙ̄	
3m	ⲉϥⲉⲧⲣⲉⲥⲥⲱⲧⲙ̄	ⲉⲩⲉⲧⲣⲉⲥⲥⲱⲧⲙ̄
3f	ⲉⲥⲉⲧⲣⲉⲥⲥⲱⲧⲙ̄	
	ⲉϥⲉ—ⲧⲣⲉ—ⲧⲉⲥϩⲓⲙⲉ ⲥⲱⲧⲙ̄	

	Negative	
	Singular	Plural
1	ⲛ̄ⲛⲁⲧⲣⲉⲥⲥⲱⲧⲙ̄	ⲛ̄ⲛⲉⲛⲧⲣⲉⲥⲥⲱⲧⲙ̄
2m	ⲛ̄ⲛⲉⲕⲧⲣⲉⲥⲥⲱⲧⲙ̄	ⲛ̄ⲛⲉⲧⲛ̄ⲧⲣⲉⲥⲥⲱⲧⲙ̄
2f	ⲛ̄ⲛⲉⲧⲣⲉⲥⲥⲱⲧⲙ̄	
3m	ⲛ̄ⲛⲉϥⲧⲣⲉⲥⲥⲱⲧⲙ̄	ⲛ̄ⲛⲉⲩⲧⲣⲉⲥⲥⲱⲧⲙ
3f	ⲛ̄ⲛⲉⲥⲧⲣⲉⲥⲥⲱⲧⲙ̄	
	ⲛ̄ⲛⲉϥ—ⲧⲣⲉ—ⲧⲉⲥϩⲓⲙⲉ ⲥⲱⲧⲙ̄	

Injunctive (Causative Imperative or Optative)

	Positive	
	Singular	Plural
	___________	___________

	Negative	
	Singular	Plural
1	ⲙ̄ⲡⲣ̄ⲧⲣⲁⲥⲱⲧⲙ̄	ⲙ̄ⲡⲣ̄ⲧⲣⲉⲛⲥⲱⲧⲙ̄
2m	________	________
2f	________	________
3m	ⲙ̄ⲡⲣ̄ⲧⲣⲉϥⲥⲱⲧⲙ̄	ⲙ̄ⲡⲣ̄ⲧⲣⲉⲩⲥⲱⲧⲙ̄
3f	ⲙ̄ⲡⲣ̄ⲧⲣⲉⲥⲥⲱⲧⲙ̄	
	ⲙ̄ⲡⲣ̄ⲧⲣⲉ—ⲧⲉⲥϩⲓⲙⲉ ⲥⲱⲧⲙ̄	

Clause or Subordinate Clause Conjugations

Temporal

	Positive	
	Singular	Plural
1	ⲛ̄ⲧⲉⲣⲓⲧⲣⲉⲥⲥⲱⲧⲙ̄	ⲛ̄ⲧⲉⲣⲛ̄ⲧⲣⲉⲥⲥⲱⲧⲙ̄
2m	ⲛ̄ⲧⲉⲣⲉⲕⲧⲣⲉⲥⲥⲱⲧⲙ̄	ⲛ̄ⲧⲉⲣⲉⲧⲛ̄ⲧⲣⲉⲥⲥⲱⲧⲙ̄
2f	ⲛ̄ⲧⲉⲣⲉⲧⲣⲉⲥⲥⲱⲧⲙ̄	
3m	ⲛ̄ⲧⲉⲣⲉϥⲧⲣⲉⲥⲥⲱⲧⲙ̄	ⲛ̄ⲧⲉⲣⲟⲩⲧⲣⲉⲥⲥⲱⲧⲙ̄
3f	ⲛ̄ⲧⲉⲣⲉⲥⲧⲣⲉⲥⲥⲱⲧⲙ̄	

ⲛ̄ⲧⲉⲣⲉϥ—ⲧⲣⲉ–ⲧⲉⲥϩⲓⲙⲉ ⲥⲱⲧⲙ̄

Conditional

	Positive	
	Singular	Plural
1	ⲉⲓϣⲁⲛⲧⲣⲉϥⲥⲱⲧⲙ̄	ⲉⲛϣⲁⲛⲧⲣⲉϥⲥⲱⲧⲙ̄
2m	ⲉⲕϣⲁⲛⲧⲣⲉϥⲥⲱⲧⲙ̄	ⲉⲧⲉⲧⲛ̄ϣⲁⲛⲧⲣⲉϥⲥⲱⲧⲙ̄
2f	ⲉⲣⲉϣⲁⲛⲧⲣⲉϥⲥⲱⲧⲙ̄	
3m	ⲉϥϣⲁⲛⲧⲣⲣⲉϥⲥⲱⲧⲙ̄	ⲉⲩϣⲁⲛⲧⲣⲉϥⲥⲱⲧⲙ̄
3f	ⲉⲥϣⲁⲛⲧⲣⲉϥⲥⲱⲧⲙ̄	

ⲉⲥϣⲁⲛ—ⲧⲣⲉ–ⲡⲣⲱⲙⲉ ⲥⲱⲧⲙ̄

"Until"

	Positive	
	Singular	Plural
1	ϣⲁⲛϯⲧⲣⲉⲥⲥⲱⲧⲙ̄	ϣⲁⲛⲧⲛ̄ⲧⲣⲉⲥⲥⲱⲧⲙ̄
2m	ϣⲁⲛⲧⲕ̄ⲧⲣⲉⲥⲥⲱⲧⲙ̄	ϣⲁⲛⲧⲉⲧⲛ̄ⲧⲣⲉⲥⲥⲱⲧⲙ̄
2f	ϣⲁⲛⲧⲉⲧⲣⲉⲥⲥⲱⲧⲙ̄	
3m	ϣⲁⲛⲧϥ̄ⲧⲣⲉⲥⲥⲱⲧⲙ̄	ϣⲁⲛⲧⲟⲩⲧⲣⲉⲥⲥⲱⲧⲙ̄
3f	ϣⲁⲛⲧⲥ̄ⲧⲣⲉⲥⲥⲱⲧⲙ̄	

ϣⲁⲛⲧⲉϥ— ⲧⲣⲉ–ⲧⲉⲥϩⲓⲙⲉ ⲥⲱⲧⲙ̄

Conjunctive

	Positive	
	Singular	Plural
1	(ⲛ̅)ⲧⲁⲧⲣⲉⲥⲥⲱⲧⲙ̅	ⲛ̅ⲧⲛ̅ⲧⲣⲉⲥ̅ⲥⲱⲧⲙ̅
2m	ⲛⲅ̅ⲧⲣⲉⲥⲥⲱⲧⲙ̅[57]	ⲛ̅ⲧⲉⲧⲛ̅ⲧⲣⲉⲥ̅ⲥⲱⲧⲙ̅
2f	ⲛ̅ⲧⲉⲧⲣⲉⲥⲥⲱⲧⲙ̅	
3m	ⲛϥ̅ⲧⲣⲉϥⲥⲱⲧⲙ̅[57]	ⲛ̅ⲥⲉⲧⲣⲉⲥⲥⲱⲧⲙ̅
3f	ⲛⲥ̅ⲧⲣⲉⲥⲥⲱⲧⲙ̅[57]	
	ⲛϥ̅— ⲧⲣⲉ–ⲧⲉⲥϩⲓⲙⲉ ⲥⲱⲧⲙ̅	

Future Conjunctive of Result (*Finalis*)

	Positive	
	Singular	Plural
1	ⲧⲁⲣⲓⲧⲣⲉⲥⲥⲱⲧⲙ̅	ⲧⲁⲣⲛ̅ⲧⲣⲉⲥⲥⲱⲧⲙ̅
2m	ⲧⲁⲣⲉⲕⲧⲣⲉⲥⲥⲱⲧⲙ̅	ⲧⲁⲣⲉⲧⲛ̅ⲧⲣⲉⲥⲥⲱⲧⲙ̅
2f	ⲧⲁⲣⲉⲧⲣⲉⲥⲥⲱⲧⲙ̅	
3m	ⲧⲁⲣⲉϥⲧⲣⲉⲥⲥⲱⲧⲙ̅	ⲧⲁⲣⲟⲩⲧⲣⲉⲥⲥⲱⲧⲙ̅
3f	ⲧⲁⲣⲉⲥⲧⲣⲉⲥⲥⲱⲧⲙ̅	
	ⲧⲁⲣⲉϥ–ⲧⲣⲉ— ⲧⲉⲥϩⲓⲙⲉ ⲥⲱⲧⲙ̅	

The Bipartite or Durative Pattern

First Present

	Positive	
	Singular	Plural
1	ϯⲧⲣⲉⲩⲥⲱⲧⲙ̅	ⲧⲛ̅ⲧⲣⲉⲩⲥⲱⲧⲙ̅
2m	ⲕⲧⲣⲉⲩⲥⲱⲧⲙ̅	ⲧⲉⲧⲛ̅ⲧⲣⲉⲩⲥⲱⲧⲙ̅
2f	ⲧⲉⲧⲣⲉⲩⲥⲱⲧⲙ̅[58]	
3m	ϥⲧⲣⲉⲩⲥⲱⲧⲙ̅	ⲥⲉⲧⲣⲉⲩⲥⲱⲧⲙ̅
3f	ⲥⲧⲣⲉⲩⲥⲱⲧⲙ̅	
	ⲥ—ⲧⲣⲉ—ⲛ̅ⲣⲱⲙⲉ ⲥⲱⲧⲙ̅	

[57] The superlinear stroke may also appear over the ⲛ̅ rather than shifting in the second masculine singular and third person singular forms, e.g., ⲛ̅ⲅⲥⲱⲧⲙ̅, ⲛ̅ϥⲥⲱⲧⲙ̅, and ⲛ̅ⲥⲥⲱⲧⲙ̅.

[58] Variant ⲧⲣ̅ⲧⲣⲉⲩ̈ⲥⲱⲧⲙ̅.

Imperfect
(=Preterit First Present)

	Positive	
	Singular	Plural
1	ⲛⲉⲓⲧⲣⲉⲩⲥⲱⲧⲙ̅ (ⲡⲉ)	ⲛⲉⲛⲧⲣⲉⲩⲥⲱⲧⲙ̅ (ⲡⲉ)
2m	ⲛⲉⲕⲧⲣⲉⲩⲥⲱⲧⲙ̅ (ⲡⲉ)	ⲛⲉⲧⲉⲧⲛ̅ⲧⲣⲉⲩⲥⲱⲧⲙ̅ (ⲡⲉ)
2f	ⲛⲉⲣⲉⲧⲣⲉⲩⲥⲱⲧⲙ̅ (ⲡⲉ)	
3m	ⲛⲉϥⲧⲣⲉⲩⲥⲱⲧⲙ̅ (ⲡⲉ)	ⲛⲉⲩⲧⲣⲉⲩⲥⲱⲧⲙ̅ (ⲡⲉ)
3f	ⲛⲉⲥⲧⲣⲉⲩⲥⲱⲧⲙ̅ (ⲡⲉ)	
	ⲛⲉϥ–ⲧⲣⲉ—ⲛ̅ⲣⲱⲙⲉ ⲥⲱⲧⲙ̅	
	ⲛⲉⲩⲛ̅ⲧⲁϥ–ⲧⲣⲉ– ϩⲉⲛⲣⲱⲙⲉ ⲥⲱⲧⲙ̅[59]	

First Future

	Positive	
	Singular	Plural
1	ϯⲛⲁⲧⲣⲉϥⲥⲱⲧⲙ̅	ⲧⲛ̅ⲛⲁⲧⲣⲉϥⲥⲱⲧⲙ̅
2m	ⲕⲛⲁⲧⲣⲉϥⲥⲱⲧⲙ̅	ⲧⲉⲧⲛ̅ⲛⲁⲧⲣⲉϥⲥⲱⲧⲙ̅
2f	ⲧⲉⲛⲁⲧⲣⲉϥⲥⲱⲧⲙ̅[60]	
3m	ϥⲛⲁⲧⲣⲉϥⲥⲱⲧⲙ̅	ⲥⲉⲛⲁⲧⲣⲉϥⲥⲱⲧⲙ̅
3f	ⲥⲛⲁⲧⲣⲉϥⲥⲱⲧⲙ̅	
	ⲥⲛⲁ—ⲧⲣⲉ—ⲡⲣⲱⲙⲉ ⲥⲱⲧⲙ̅	

	Negative	
	Singular	Plural
1	ϯⲛⲁⲧⲙ̅ⲧⲣⲉϥⲥⲱⲧⲙ̅	ⲧⲛ̅ⲛⲁⲧⲙ̅ⲧⲣⲉϥⲥⲱⲧⲙ̅
2m	ⲕⲛⲁⲧⲙ̅ⲧⲣⲉϥⲥⲱⲧⲙ̅	ⲧⲉⲧⲛ̅ⲛⲁⲧⲙ̅ⲧⲣⲉϥⲥⲱⲧⲙ̅
2f	ⲧⲉⲛⲁⲧⲙ̅ⲧⲣⲉϥⲥⲱⲧⲙ̅	
3m	ϥⲛⲁⲧⲙ̅ⲧⲣⲉϥⲥⲱⲧⲙ̅	ⲥⲉⲛⲁⲧⲙ̅ⲧⲣⲉϥⲥⲱⲧⲙ̅
3f	ⲥⲛⲁⲧⲙ̅ⲧⲣⲉϥⲥⲱⲧⲙ̅	
	ⲥⲛⲁ–ⲧⲙ̅—ⲧⲣⲉ—ⲡⲣⲱⲙⲉ ⲥⲱⲧⲙ̅	

[59] ⲛⲉⲩⲛ̅ⲧⲁϥ– is contracted from ⲛⲉ–ⲟⲩⲛ̅ⲧⲁϥ.
[60] Variant ⲧⲣ̅ⲛⲁⲧⲣⲉϥⲥⲱⲧⲙ̅.